NEW CLAIT
OCR LEVEL 1 CERTIFICATE FOR IT USERS

VERONICA WHITE

Heinemann

OCR
RECOGNISING ACHIEVEMENT

Heinemann Educational Publishers
Halley Court, Jordan Hill, Oxford, OX2 8EJ
Part of Harcourt Education

Heinemann is the registered trademark of Harcourt Education Limited

First published in 2002
2005 2004 2003
10 9 8 7 6 5 4

A catalogue record for this book is available from the British Library on request.

IBSN 0 435 45558 3

Designed and typeset by Artistix, Thame, Oxon.
Printed and bound in Spain by Edelvives.

Tel: 01865 888058 www.heinemann.co.uk

Acknowledgements
I would like to thank my daughter, Kate, for her continuing inspiration and Pen Gresford and Alex Gray for their support, wisdom and knowledge.

The publishers would also like to thank Paul Baxter from Tropical Places for the use of the web page on pages 5 and 104.

Screenshots reprinted with permission from Microsoft Corporation.

Contents

Introduction
The NEW CLAIT Applications

The scheme

OCR's Level 1 Certificate for IT Users (NEW CLAIT) is an OCR scheme that provides opportunities for you to be assessed in the use of computers and information technology.

The book

The book is designed to help you to understand how computers can process information in a number of ways. It will introduce you to the skills required to operate a variety of computer application packages.

The skills you practise and acquire are becoming essential for everyday life and will provide you with the foundation for many forms of employment and leisure activities.

The book has been written primarily for the OCR Level 1 Certificate for IT Users (NEW CLAIT) scheme but it can be used by anyone who wants a practical introduction to computers and information technology.

You may be using this book with or without the help of a teacher or tutor. If you are working alone you will need to refer to your computer manual to find out the exact instructions for your machine. The book cannot give you these instructions because of the very many different types of computer equipment and programs that are used.

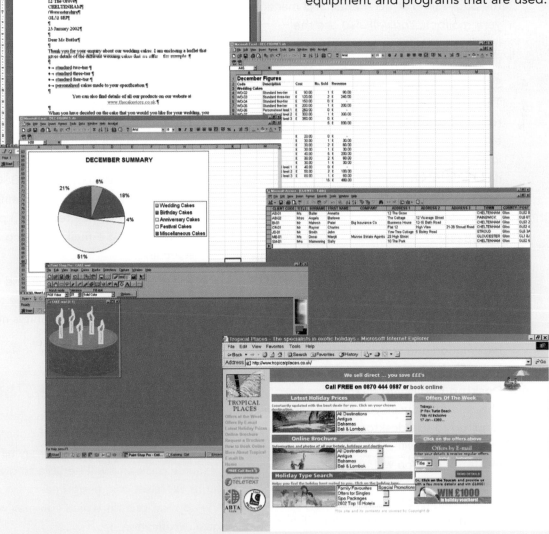

The units in OCR's Level 1 Certificate for IT Users (NEW CLAIT) are described below:

1   Using a Computer

This unit introduces you to the basic skills required to use a computer and printer. You will be introduced to basic document management through use of the operating system, and you will use application software (programs) to create and print simple documents containing text and numeric data. This is the compulsory (core) unit for the full certificate.

2   Word Processing

This unit introduces you to the basic skills required to use a word processor. You will create files, key in text and save your work. You will change the text and format it in different ways. You will also print your work.

3   Electronic Communication

This unit introduces you to the basic skills required to use e-mail and browser software. You will send and receive messages (and attachments) and manage your mailbox. You will also use the Internet to search for and retrieve information. You will also print your work.

4   Spreadsheets

This unit introduces you to the basic skills required to use a spreadsheet. You will enter data into a grid and save the information. You will perform numeric calculations, change the entries you have made and format the data. You will also print your work.

5   Databases

This unit introduces you to the basic skills required to use database software. You will change entries in the database, enter new records and delete records. You will use the software to search for information and sort the data you find. You will also print your work.

6   Desktop Publishing (DTP)

This unit introduces you to the basic skills required to use desktop publishing software. You will create and save a master page. You will use prepared text and image files. You will apply different fonts and font sizes and display your work in a variety of ways. You will also print your work.

7   Graphs and Charts

This unit introduces you to the basic skills required to use data modelling software. You will transfer numeric data into graphical form (pie charts, bar charts and line graphs). You will save your graphs and you will also print your work.

8   Computer Art

This unit introduces you to the basic skills required to use computer art software. You will import prepared text, graphics and bitmapped images. You will draw shapes, use colour, change and store the images and print your artwork.

9   Web Pages

This unit introduces you to the basic skills required to use software to create simple web pages. You will use basic HTML concepts, and format your work. You will use navigation, browsing and linking techniques. You will also print your work.

10   Presentation Graphics

This unit introduces you to the basic skills required to use presentation software. You will produce a simple presentation. You will use prepared text and image files and present your work in different ways. You will also print your work.

11   BBC Becoming Webwise

This unit introduces you to the basic skills required to use digital technology and the Internet. It is in conjunction with the BBC, and is assessed via the BBC website. The on-line assessment consists of a multiple choice test and 3 practical tasks covering e-mail, browsing and searching.

You may **not** claim this unit and Unit 3 Electronic Communication due to an overlap of content. The unit is not covered in this book.

Tutor's Resource Pack

There is a Tutor's Resource Pack (also published by Heinemann) that goes with this student book. Your tutor may have that resource pack and will be able to give you more exercises and assignments for any of the applications for which you may wish to gain certification.

How To Use This Book

This book is set out in units.

Each of the units can be used independently of the others and you can use them in any order.

In each unit you will find:

- **An overview** – this is a general explanation of the application and includes brief guidance on **Helping you pass** the unit
- **Build up exercises** – these introduce you to the requirements of the OCR Level 1 Certificate for IT Users (NEW CLAIT) scheme within that application area
- **A command checklist** – this is for you to complete to form a reference sheet
- **Specimen assignments** – these will provide assessment practice and self-assessment checklists to help you to monitor your progress.

All the build up tasks and specimen assignments have numbers printed down the left-hand side. These relate to the assessment objectives in OCR's Level 1 Certificate for IT Users (NEW CLAIT) scheme for which this book is written.

Please note that the assignments included in this book must not be used as the final assessment: They are intended as practice assignments only.

The OCR Level I Certificate for IT Users (NEW CLAIT) scheme

How will you will be assessed?

Full details of the OCR syllabus can be found as a file on the CD-ROM that accompanies this book. You will be assessed in the practical use of the computer and software applications by completing assignments.

OCR prepares these assignments and you will have approximately two hours to complete each one you attempt. You can only attempt each assignment once. If you do not achieve all the assessment objectives you may attempt a different assignment.

All units are equally weighted. Neither the full certificate nor the individual units are graded other than the award of a pass.

The core unit/Unit 1 is marked by an OCR examiner-moderator. All other units are optional units and are marked by your tutor and then checked by an OCR examiner-moderator. Computer-based assessment is to be made available to all centres for the most popular units of the scheme.

Structure of the units

Each unit is structured as follows:

- **Learning outcomes** – what you can expect to know having followed a programme of learning designed to prepare you for this unit
- **Assessment objectives** – the skills you will have to demonstrate during the assessment. The assessment objectives are grouped under the learning outcomes
- **Knowledge and understanding** – what you need to know before you start on the exercises.

How many applications are you required to do?

You can attempt any number of the units from just one to all. You may choose the units that reflect your own needs or interests.

To gain a full certificate you are required to achieve 5 units – the core unit plus 4 optional units. Units may be achieved and certificated separately.

How can you be successful?

The syllabus clearly identifies the work you will have to do. You should complete the assignments with **no** critical errors, and not more than 3 **accuracy** errors. Errors corrected on/before the final print should **not** be penalised.

Critical errors

A critical error renders the work unfit for its purpose. The critical errors for each unit are:

UNIT TITLE	CRITICAL ERRORS
Using a Computer	Failing to amend or print the specified document in any way Failing to create the new document
Word Processing	Not carrying out an edit – insert, move, delete, replace – but note that edits not carried out correctly are penalised as accuracy errors
Electronic Communication	An incorrect or omitted e-mail address A missing or incorrect attachment Failing to locate and print specified web pages
Spreadsheets	Failing to generate and display correct results Failing to delete/insert specified row/column
Databases	Incorrect search results Missing field(s)
Desktop Publishing	A missing image Imported text file is incomplete
Graphs and Charts	Incorrect or missing data on graph/chart Unusable legend or labels (ie not clearly and accurately identified)
Computer Art	A missing or incorrect image A missing block of text
Web Pages	A link that does not load the correct page or generate the correctly addressed e-mail message A missing image
Presentation Graphics	A missing image A missing slide

Accuracy errors

An accuracy error is one that does not prevent the work from being used, and may occur in two different ways.

- **Errors in completing assessment objectives**
  It will be considered as an error if you do not achieve an assessment objective as specified. One error is incurred **each** time an objective is not met (even if the objective is tested more than once. You should not be penalised for failing to achieve an objective if this is as a result of an earlier error (eg a data entry error causes a search to be incomplete).
- **Errors in keying data (data entry errors)**
  A data entry error is an incorrect, omitted, or extra character in a data item or an omitted or extra space. Only one data entry error should be counted for a data item, regardless of the number of errors in the data item.

Note: The data item varies in scope for each unit, depending partly upon the relative importance of data accuracy. The list below defines a data item for each unit:

UNIT TITLE	DATA ITEM
Using a Computer	individual characters in the keyed-in document
Word Processing	a word
Electronic Communication	a subject heading or a word in the body of the message
Spreadsheets	the contents of a cell
Databases	the contents of a field
Desktop Publishing	the heading
Graphs and Charts	an entire label, heading or title
Computer Art	an entire item of text
Web Pages	a word, or a line of link text
Presentation Graphics	a line of text

In many of units you must add your name, centre number and the date to your work. These details are **not** assessed for accuracy. Omission of any of this data is penalised **once only per assessment** as a single accuracy error.

A word is any normally recognisable word (hyphenated words count as one), or any series of characters that constitute a recognisable unit such as numbers (eg 339) or dates (eg 28/9/48), and includes the space following the word and any associated punctuation.

What certificate will you get?

If you achieve the core unit (Unit 1) plus 4 optional units you will be awarded an OCR Level 1 Certificate for IT Users (NEW CLAIT). You will receive a certificate that lists the units achieved.

If you achieve fewer than the number of units required for a full qualification you will be awarded a unit certificate for each unit achieved.

About the CD-ROM

The accompanying CD-ROM contains all the files that you will need to complete the units in this book.

Accessing the CD-ROM

To access the files on the accompanying CD-ROM, insert the CD into your CD-ROM drive and open them in the appropriate software package for each unit. It is recommended that you make a backup copy of the CD files.

Files on the CD-ROM

You will find all the files that you need to use in this book on the CD. The files for each unit are stored in a folder/directory indicating that unit – eg the files for Unit 1 (Using a computer) are in the folder Unit1.

You will be told within each task the name of the file (or files) that you must use.

Please note that in Unit 2 (Word processing), and Unit 4 (Spreadsheets) the data is **keyed in**, not loaded from disk.

UNIT 1 Using A Computer Overview

What is this unit about?

This unit is about the tasks you need to carry out whatever system or program you are using – ie the basic skills.

Although each of the NEW CLAIT applications serves a different purpose you will need to be able to carry out some basic operations within any application that you use.

So what are these tasks? To use any of the applications you will have to learn how to:

- use a computer and printer
- locate and access data on a computer
- input and import text, numbers and symbols
- print
- manage files.

Why use a computer system?

A computer system allows you to enter, process, save and print your work. Computer systems offer you the opportunity to update, edit or change information stored without the need to enter all the information again.

Once entered into the computer system, information can be manipulated. For example, in word processing the layout of the page can be changed; in spreadsheets, calculations can be performed; in desktop publishing, you may change the font from serif to sans-serif. You can also search and sort the information quickly and accurately.

What is a computer system?

A computer system consists of:

- **Hardware components:**
  - *Input* – to enter instructions and data, such as a keyboard, mouse, voice input, downloading from the Internet, importing files or by scanning.
  - *Processor* – to carry out the instructions.
  - *Output* – to provide hard copy, such as from a printer or plotter.
- **Software:**
  - *Operating system* – the basic programs that make the computer work, such as DOS and Windows. Windows is a 'visual' version of DOS. It operates by the use of menus, icons and toolbars. It includes 'utilities' such as 'find file'.
  - *Application programs* – programs that are designed for a particular purpose, such as word processing, electronic communication, spreadsheets, databases, desktop publishing, graphs and charts, computer art, web pages, and presentation graphics.

Switching on your computer system and loading an application

You must be sure that you switch on all the necessary parts of your computer system and load the application program in the correct sequence.

You should be familiar with the use of passwords to gain access to the system. A password may be required either through the system or network login procedure, or through a password-protected datafile. The use will depend on the needs of the system and its users. Many companies protect data at file level, including the restriction on a user's access (eg ability to amend a file, or read only).

It is good practice when choosing a password not to use an *obvious* selection (such as your name, or other personal details). Many systems have automatic reminders to change your password. This is also good practice and you are again advised not to use obvious entries (such as months of the year).

Input text, numbers and symbols

It is essential that you enter data accurately otherwise the value of the information produced will not be satisfactory.

Printing

Producing output from your computer requires the use of (mainly) a printer. You should know how to operate your printer and how to change the consumables, such as paper and print cartridges or toner.

Managing documents and data

Open an existing document

You need to know the name of the file you want to recall and where it is stored. If you do not know the file location you can use the **find file** facility.

Save an existing document

Your work can be saved on disk so that you can recall it later. It is essential that you save your work frequently. If you do not, and there is a problem such that the computer system ceases to operate, then you can only recall the last saved version of your work.

You will need to give the file a unique name, ie a name that is different from any other file in the storage area you are going to use. Care should be taken to select a suitable name that will help you to identify the contents at a later date. Some systems will have a restriction on the number and type of characters that can be used as filenames.

Copying and backing up a file or disk

Both of these commands allow you to have a second copy of files (or entire folders, directories or disks). This is a security measure and the second copy should be stored in a safe and separate place.

Copying allows you to make a second version of a file. This may be on another disk or in a different directory or folder. Using the **save as** command allows you to make a copy of a file using a different name.

If you use the backup command the file will be condensed to save disk space. You have to restore your file before being able to use it again.

Delete a file

This will allow you to delete or erase a file containing information you no longer require.

Closing down the application and exiting the system

You should always be certain that you have saved your work, particularly if you have made changes or entered new data. Make sure that you follow the instructions for exiting the application program and that you switch off all parts of the computer system.

Other useful utilities

To make the best use of your computer system it is also helpful to be able to:

View or list the contents of a disk

This will provide a list, catalogue or directory of all the files stored in that location.

Format a blank floppy disk

Most new floppy disks are blank and need to have a series of magnetic tracks put onto them to prepare the disk for storing data. You will need to use a formatting program. Once the disk has been formatted it will not require formatting again unless you wish to use it on a different system. If you format a disk which already has data stored on it, you will lose all that data.

Disk and file care

A disk is the storage medium and a file is the collection of information stored on disk.

Care should be taken with disks: avoid touching the surface, keep away from magnetic sources, warm places, dust and liquids. Use a felt pen to write on the disk label if it is already on the disk, to avoid damage to the contents. Better still, write the label before sticking it on the disk. Store disks in a protective box or wallet.

Helping you pass

Critical errors

- Failing to amend or print the specified document in any way.
- Failing to create the new document.

Accuracy errors

- Check the data that you have entered in the new document as **each missing, incorrect or extra character** will count as a separate accuracy error.
- Check that you have completed all the objectives as each one not met will count as a separate error.

Tips

- In the OCR assignment you will be given filenames and you *must* use the specified filenames.
- Your personal details *must* be entered (they will not be assessed for accuracy).

Build Up Exercises

TASK 1

This task is designed to allow you to practise the skills required to gain OCR Level 1 Certificate for IT Users (NEW CLAIT) assessment objectives.

Before you begin

You will need to find out and note down how to:

- switch on your computer and monitor safely
- gain access to data using a login and/or password
- navigate the operating system
- use file search facilities

- find a specified file
- load application software
- open an existing document file
- use an input device to enter data
- enter text, numbers and symbols
- save an existing document.

There is a checklist for you to complete on page 15, to use as a reference sheet.

You should begin this task with the computer workstation and printer switched off. You must use a password to gain access to the data. You will need access to the file **agenda312**.

The file **agenda312** is supplied as a Word document on the CD supplied with this book. You should use the 'find file' facility (or equivalent) to locate it.

Scenario

You are starting a new job as an administrator. You have been asked to demonstrate your computer skills by working through the following task.

What You Have To Do		
Assessment Objectives		**Your computer is ready for use. Your tutor will give you a password to gain access to the system.**
1a, 2a	1	Switch on the computer and monitor correctly and safely. Wait for the operating system software to load fully.
1c, 2b, 2c	2	Using the operating system's 'find file' or 'search' facility, find the text file **agenda312**.
1d, 5b	3	Using an application that will allow you to read text files, open the file in the application.
1e, 3a, 3b 3c	4	Using the mouse and keyboard (or alternatives if available) add your name, centre number and today's date at the end of the file.
5c	5	Save the document using the original filename **agenda312**.

This task is designed to allow you to practise the skills required to gain OCR Level 1 Certificate for IT Users (NEW CLAIT) assessment objectives.

Before you begin

You will need to find out and note down how to:

- use a personal computer and printer to produce a document
- switch on your printer safely
- load paper
- print a document
- close a document.

What You Have To Do

Assessment Objectives		
4a, 4b	1	Switch on your printer and load paper.
1b, 4c	2	Print the document **agenda312** using the default printer settings.
5e	3	Close the document **agenda312**.

This task is designed to allow you to practise the skills required to gain OCR Level 1 Certificate for IT Users (NEW CLAIT) assessment objectives.

Before you begin

You will need to find out and note down how to:

- create a new document
- save a document with a new filename.

What You Have To Do

Assessment Objectives		
5a	1	Create a new text document using the same software that you used to edit the file **agenda312**.
1e, 3a, 3b 3c	2	Enter the following data as shown, leaving a space between each line:
		a **Account no: 0045-2349-3996-1022**
		b **Exchange $ @ 2.55**
		c **Your name, centre number and today's date**
5d	3	Save this document using the filename **exchange**.
4c	4	Print the document **exchange** using the default printer settings.
5e	5	Close the document **exchange**.
1f	6	Exit the application software and shut down the operating system safely.

Using A Computer Checklist

You should complete this checklist for each hardware and software combination you use. Use information from your tutor, handouts, handbooks and software manuals to complete the list. You can then use your list as a reference sheet to complete the practice tasks that follow.

Hardware: _____

Software: _____

ASSESSMENT OBJECTIVE	HOW TO DO IT	OCR REFERENCE
1 Identify and use a computer workstation and system software		
Switch on computer and monitor safely	_____	1a
Use a personal computer and printer to produce a document	_____	1b
Navigate the operating system	_____	1c
Load application software	_____	1d
Use an input device to enter data	_____	1e
Shut down the operating system	_____	1f
2 Locate and access data on a computer		
Gain access to data using a login and/or password	_____	2a
Use file search facilities	_____	2b
Find a specified file	_____	2c
3 Input small amounts of unformatted text, numbers and symbols		
Enter text	_____	3a
Enter numbers	_____	3b
Enter symbols	_____	3c
Amend an existing document	_____	3d
4 Print a document using the default printer settings		
Switch on printer safely	_____	4a
Load paper	_____	4b
Print document	_____	4c
5 Manage documents and data		
Create a new document	_____	5a
Open an existing document	_____	5b
Save an existing document	_____	5c
Save a document with a new filename	_____	5d
Close document	_____	5e

OCR Assignments and Self-Assessments

TASK 4

This task allows you to practise a complete OCR Level 1 Certificate for IT Users (NEW CLAIT) assignment. It covers all the OCR Level 1 Certificate for IT Users (NEW CLAIT) using a computer assessment objectives.

You should begin this task with the computer workstation and printer switched off. You must use a password to gain access to the data.

You will need access to the file **memo4**.

The **memo4** file is supplied as a Word document on the CD supplied with this book. You should use the 'find file' facility (or equivalent) to locate it.

Scenario

You are starting a new job as an administrator. You have been asked to demonstrate your computer skills by working through the following task.

What You Have To Do

Assessment Objectives		Your computer is ready for use. Your tutor will give you a password to gain access to the system.
la, 2a	1	Switch on the computer and monitor correctly and safely. Wait for the operating system software to load fully.
lc, 2b, 2c	2	Using the operating system's 'find file' or 'search' facility, find the text file **memo4**.
ld, 5b	3	Using an application that will allow you to read text files, open the file in the application.
le, 3a, 3b, 3c	4	Using the mouse and keyboard (or alternatives if available) add your name, centre number and today's date at the end of the file.
5c	5	Save the document using the original filename **memo4**.
4a, 4b	6	Switch on your printer and load paper.
lb, 4c, 5e	7	Print the document **memo4** using the default printer settings, and close it.
5a	8	Create a new text document using the same software that you used to edit the file **memo4**.
le, 3a, 3b, 3c	9	Enter the following data as shown, leaving a space between each line: a JRN45@print-central.co.uk b Item No: VMX/29 – 25% discount c Your name, centre number and today's date

What You Have To Do

Assessment Objectives		
5d	10	Save this document using the filename **central4**.
4c	11	Print the document **central4** using the default printer settings.
5e	12	Close the document **central4**.
1f	13	Exit the application software and shut down the operating system safely.

Self-assessment: Task 4

Did I do it correctly?

- ☐ Switched on the computer and monitor safely

- ☐ Gained access to data using a login and/or password

- ☐ Used file search facilities and found the specified file **memo4**

- ☐ Navigated the operating system

- ☐ Loaded application software

- ☐ Opened the existing document file **memo4**

- ☐ Created a new document

- ☐ Used an input device to enter data

- ☐ Entered text, numbers and symbols

- ☐ Switched on the printer safely

- ☐ Loaded paper and printed the documents **memo4** and **central4**

- ☐ Saved an existing document **memo4**

- ☐ Saved a document with a new filename – **central4**

- ☐ Closed the documents **memo4** and **central4**

- ☐ Shut down the operating system.

TASK 5

This task allows you to practise a complete OCR Level 1 Certificate for IT Users (NEW CLAIT) assignment. It covers all the OCR Level 1 Certificate for IT Users (NEW CLAIT) using a computer assessment objectives.

You should begin this task with the computer workstation and printer switched off. You must use a password to gain access to the data.

You will need access to the file **stock**.

> The **stock** file is supplied as a Word document on the CD supplied with this book. You should use the 'find file' facility (or equivalent) to locate it.

Scenario

You are starting a new job as an administrator. You have been asked to demonstrate your computer skills by working through the following task.

What You Have To Do

Assessment Objectives		Your computer is ready for use. Your tutor will give you a password to gain access to the system.
Ia, 2a	1	Switch on the computer and monitor correctly and safely. Wait for the operating system software to load fully.
Ic, 2b, 2c	2	Using the operating system's 'find file' or 'search' facility, find the text file **stock**.
Id, 5b	3	Using an application that will allow you to read text files, open the file in the application.
Ie, 3a, 3b 3c	4	Using the mouse and keyboard (or alternatives if available) add your name, centre number and today's date at the end of the file.
5c	5	Save the document using the original filename **stock**.
4a, 4b	6	Switch on your printer and load paper.
Ib, 4c	7	Print the document **stock** using the default printer settings.
5e	8	Close the document **stock**.
5a	9	Create a new text document using the same software that you used to edit the file **stock**.
Ie, 3a, 3b 3c	10	Enter the following data as shown, leaving a space between each line: a **Catalogue nos: 0399-3A to 2399-3A** b **Discount: 45%** c **Your name, centre number and today's date**
5d	11	Save this document using the filename **cat3a**.
4c	12	Print the document using the default printer settings.
5e	13	Close the document **cat3a**.
If	14	Exit the application software and shut down the operating system safely.

Self-assessment: Task 5

Did I do it correctly?

❏ Switched on the computer and monitor safely

❏ Gained access to data using a login and/or password

❏ Used file search facilities and found a specified file

❏ Navigated the operating system

❏ Loaded application software

❏ Opened an existing document

❏ Created a new document

❏ Used an input device to enter data

❏ Entered text, numbers and symbols

❏ Switched on the printer safely

❏ Loaded paper and printed documents

❏ Saved an existing document

❏ Saved a document with a new filename

❏ Closed documents

❏ Shut down the operating system.

UNIT 2 Word Processing Overview

What is word processing?

Word processing allows you to enter text into a computer system. Both the text and its appearance can be altered. Changes in the text are referred to as editing and amending, changes in appearance are referred to as formatting. The text can be stored on disk, recalled later and printed out when required.

Why use a word processing system?

Using a word processing system will allow you to enter text and correct any errors or make any changes required without the need to re-key the whole document. Your information can be saved on disk and recalled later and you can print as required.

Text input

New text is input from prepared information and notes or you can compose directly. Text previously saved on disk can be recalled and added to or amended as required. Text can also be 'captured' by use of voice recognition packages and scanning devices.

Processing of information

The text can be edited and formatted as required.

Editing

This term covers the variety of operations (such as insert, delete, move or search and replace) which you use to make changes and corrections to text on the screen.

Text formatting

This term covers a variety of operations which change the layout and appearance of the text. It includes changing the margins, alignment, centring and emboldening text.

Printing final copy

A copy of the text stored in the system can be printed out on your printer. You will need to be sure that your word processing system recognises the printer that is attached. The quality of the hard copy (output from the computer printed on paper) will depend on the type and quality of printer used.

Word processing actions

Editing

Insert

You can insert new text at any point by moving the cursor to the appropriate position and keying in the new text.

Delete

There are several methods of deleting text. You can delete an individual character or a few characters by moving the cursor to the appropriate point and then using the delete to the left or delete to the right key. If you wish to delete larger amounts of text you should identify the block to be deleted, and issue the instruction to delete the block.

Move

This function allows you to move a phrase, paragraph or block of text from one position in the document to another.

Replace

This function allows one word or phrase to be exchanged for another. The instruction can apply to just one occurrence, to a specified number of occurrences or every time the word or phrase occurs in the document. You will need to specify the word or phrase to be replaced, followed by the new text required.

Formatting

Margins

You can change the position of the left-hand margin and/or the right-hand margin. The changes in margins may be given to your system by giving the size of the margins in inches or centimetres.

Line spacing

You can alter the line spacing, eg from single-line spacing to double-line spacing. You are able to give a block of text different line spacing within a document as well as change the line spacing for the whole document.

Justification

This function allows you to present the printed text justified or unjustified. If the justification is on then the text will be presented straight at both margins.

Text which is not right justified (ie justification is off) will appear with the right-hand text edge 'ragged'. This is also referred to as alignment.

Emphasise text

These functions allow you to **embolden**, <u>underline</u> or put the text you specify into *italics*.

Word processing terms

Default values

These are certain values for items such as the width of margin, line spacing or the alignment setting presented to you by the package when it is loaded. They are pre-programmed and will remain unchanged unless you alter them.

Word wrap

A word that is too long to fit on the end of a line is carried over to the next line without the need to enter a return.

WYSIWYG

An acronym for 'What you see is what you get'. A system is WYSIWYG if the display on the screen looks the same as the printout.

Helping you pass

Critical errors

- Not carrying out an edit – insert, move, delete, replace – but note that edits not carried out correctly are penalised as accuracy errors.

Accuracy errors

- Check the data you have entered as each **missing, incorrect or extra word** will count as a separate accuracy error.
- Check that you have completed all the objectives as each one not met will count as a separate error.

Tips

- In the OCR assignment you will be given filenames and you ***must*** use the specified filenames.
- Check the number of prints you have produced as failure to include a print will probably mean that you have not provided evidence of one or more of the objectives.

Build Up Exercises

TASK 1

This task is designed to allow you to practise the skills required to gain OCR Level 1 Certificate for IT Users (NEW CLAIT) assessment objectives.

Before you begin

You will need to find out and note down how to:

- load your word processing application and create a new document
- enter text via the keyboard, inserting paragraph breaks
- set text alignment/justification
- set margins
- enter text via the keyboard, inserting paragraph breaks
- save and print a document

There is a checklist for you to complete on page 25 to use as a reference sheet.

What You Have To Do

Assessment Objectives		
1a, 5a	1	Start up your word processing system and open a new file.
4a	2	Set the left and right page margins to 2.5 cm.
2a, 3d	3	Enter the following text with an unjustified right margin and a justified left margin.

HELP WITH FINANCE

Most companies now use computers to make sure that they remain in control of their finances. Use of financial packages gives you more control, and allows for analysis and flexibility when dealing with your finances.

The advent of 24-hour access has made banking much easier. This access allows you to check your accounts and balances, view specified transactions, make transfers between accounts and pay bills.

Getting the answer to any of your financial queries and fulfilling your daily needs is now easier than ever before. You can use guides which provide tips, information and guidance on topics such as opening a company, trading on the Internet and keeping your company afloat.

You can get advice on issues such as how you can reduce your bank charges and the methods to use to develop company strategies. Basic book-keeping and production planning are also covered. You can also view direct debits and standing orders, request statements, cheque books and paying-in books. You no longer need to worry about understanding effective marketing.

2a	4	Enter your name, centre number and today's date a few lines below the end of the text.
5b, 5d	5	Save the text and print one copy.

TASK **2**

This task is designed to allow you to practise the skills required to gain OCR Level 1 Certificate for IT Users (NEW CLAIT) assessment objectives.

Before you begin

You will need to find out and note down how to:

- insert text
- move text
- change font
- change font size
- emphasise text
- insert paragraph breaks
- save document using a new filename.

What You Have To Do

Assessment Objectives		
	I	Reload the text saved in Task 1.
3a	2	Change *only* the heading **HELP WITH FINANCE** to a different font.
3b	3	Change the size of the heading **HELP WITH FINANCE** so that it is larger than the rest of the text.
3c, 3d	4	Embolden and centre the heading **HELP WITH FINANCE**. Make sure that the rest of the text is not emboldened.
3d	5	Fully justify all the text (apart from the heading).
2b	6	Insert a new paragraph after the paragraph beginning **… The advent of 24-hour …** **Many banks offer unlimited Internet access which is free, other than the cost of a local call. The packages also include e-mail facilities to help you keep in touch with suppliers and customers.**
4b	7	Insert a paragraph break and clear line space in the last paragraph after the words **… production planning are also covered.**
2c	8	Move the sentence shown below which appears in the final paragraph so that it becomes the last sentence in the second paragraph. **You can also view direct debits and standing orders, request statements, cheque books and paying-in books.**
5c, 5d	9	Save the file using a new filename, and print one copy.

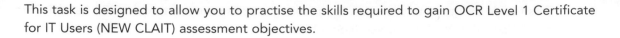

TASK 3

This task is designed to allow you to practise the skills required to gain OCR Level 1 Certificate for IT Users (NEW CLAIT) assessment objectives.

Before you begin

You will need to find out and note down how to:

- delete text
- replace specified text
- amend margins
- change the left margin
- change the right margin
- change the line spacing
- close your file.

What You Have To Do

Assessment Objectives		
2d	1	In the paragraph beginning **You can get advice on issues ...** delete the sentence **... Basic book-keeping and production planning are also covered**.
2e	2	The word **company** appears three times. Replace the word **company** with the word **business** each time it appears.
4a	3	Change the left and right margins from 2.5 cm to 2 cm.
4c	4	Set the whole document in double-line spacing.
5b, 5c	5	Save your file and print a copy.
1a, 5d, 5e	6	Close your file and the word processing application in the correct sequence, making sure that the data is secure.

Word Processing Checklist

You should complete this checklist for each hardware and software combination you use. Use information from your tutor, handouts, handbooks and software manuals to complete the list. You can then use your list as a reference sheet to complete the practice tasks that follow.

Hardware: _____

Software: _____

ASSESSMENT OBJECTIVE	HOW TO DO IT	OCR REFERENCE
1 Identify and use word processing software correctly		
Use appropriate application software	_____	1a
2 Use an input device to enter and edit text accurately		
Enter text in paragraphs	_____	2a
Insert text	_____	2b
Move text	_____	2c
Delete text	_____	2d
Replace specified text	_____	2e
3 Select fonts and simple text formatting		
Change font	_____	3a
Change font size	_____	3b
Emphasise text		
bold	_____	3c
italic	_____	3c
underline	_____	3c
Set text alignment	_____	3d
Set justification ON/OFF	_____	3d
4 Format basic paragraph and document properties		
Set/amend margins	_____	4a
Insert paragraph breaks	_____	4b
Amend line spacing	_____	4c
5 Manage and print word processing documents		
Create a new document	_____	5a
Save document	_____	5b
Save document with new filename	_____	5c
Print document	_____	5d
Close document	_____	5e

OCR Assignments and Self-Assessments

TASK 4

This task allows you to practise a complete OCR Level 1 Certificate for IT Users (NEW CLAIT) assignment. It covers all the OCR Level 1 Certificate for IT Users (NEW CLAIT) word processing assessment objectives.

What You Have To Do

Assessment Objectives		What You Have To Do
1a, 5a	1	Start up your word processing system and open a new file.
4a	2	Set the left and right page margins to 2 cm.
2a, 3d	3	Enter the following text using an unjustified right-hand margin and a justified left margin.

AIR TRAFFIC JAMS

Predictions of bottlenecks and air space problems abound. Travellers on commercial airlines are being warned to expect delays as Europe's air space congestion builds. Solutions are being put forward by airlines, aviation bodies and governmental groups.

The most important step forward would appear to be to consider the sky above Europe as one common air space. Suggestions include opening up air space currently restricted to military use to create extra space for commercial aircraft. At present each country controls its own air territory, but there are benefits to be gained if the total space is managed as one area. Standards will have to be put in place to ensure safety, and reflect performance and cost considerations.

One way that passengers may choose to try and avoid bottlenecks over European air space in the future is by opting to use smaller airports. Point-to-point travel between the larger airports means a likelihood of encountering air space congestion. Use of smaller airports continues to rise.

Assessment Objectives		What You Have To Do
2a	4	Enter your name, centre number and today's date a few lines below the end of the text.
5b, 5d	5	Check through your work thoroughly and correct any errors you may have made. Save your document and print one copy.

What You Have To Do

Assessment Objectives		
3a	6	Change *only* the heading **AIR TRAFFIC JAMS** to a different font.
3b	7	Change the size of the heading **AIR TRAFFIC JAMS** so that it is larger than the rest of the text.
3c, 3d	8	Embolden and centre the heading **AIR TRAFFIC JAMS**. Make sure that the rest of the text is not emboldened.
3d	9	Fully justify all the text (apart from the heading).
2b	10	Insert a new paragraph after the first paragraph.
		A working group of commercial and military officials has been established to look at proposals for change within the EC. Many within the industry believe that the problems with congestion will not be resolved in less than ten years.
4b	11	Insert a paragraph break and clear line space in the paragraph beginning **... The most important step** after the words **... extra space for commercial aircraft**.
2c	12	Move the sentence shown below which appears in the third paragraph so that it becomes the last sentence in the first paragraph.
		Suggestions include opening up air space currently restricted to military use to create extra space for commercial aircraft.
2d	13	In the final paragraph delete the sentence **... Point-to-point travel between the larger airports means a likelihood of encountering air space congestion.**
2e	14	The word **commercial** appears three times. Replace the word **commercial** with the word **civilian** each time it appears.
5c	15	Save the file using a new filename.
4c	16	Reload the file saved with the new filename. Set the whole document in double-line spacing.
4a	17	Change the left and right margins from 2 cm to 3 cm.
1a, 5d, 5e	18	Print the document, close your file and the word processing application in the correct sequence, making sure that the data is secure.

Self-assessment: Task 4

Did I do it correctly?

☐ Switched on the computer system and loaded the word processing program

☐ Entered the text

☐ Saved the text

☐ Inserted the new paragraph

A working group of commercial and military officials has been established to look at proposals for change within the EC. Many within the industry believe that the problems with congestion will not be resolved in less than ten years.

☐ Deleted the sentence

Point-to-point travel between the larger airports means a likelihood of encountering air space congestion.

☐ Moved the sentence so that it became the last sentence in the first paragraph

Suggestions include opening up air space currently restricted to military use to create extra space for commercial aircraft.

☐ Replaced the 3 occurrences of **commercial** with **civilian**

☐ Changed the right-hand and left-hand margin widths

☐ Changed the line spacing from single to double

☐ Produced text that was unjustified and then changed it to fully justified text

☐ Emphasised, centred and changed the font and font size of the heading

☐ Printed the document three times

☐ Saved the work with a new filename

☐ Saved the file when work finished

☐ Closed down the word processing system with the data safely saved.

TASK 5

This task allows you to practise a complete OCR Level 1 Certificate for IT Users (NEW CLAIT) assignment. It covers all the OCR Level 1 Certificate for IT Users (NEW CLAIT) Word Processing assessment objectives.

What You Have To Do

Assessment Objectives		
1a, 5a	1	Start up your word processing system and open a new file.
2a, 3a, 3b	2	Enter the following text using the font Times New Roman, size 14.
3c, 3d.		Use single-line spacing with an unjustified right-hand margin. Centre and
4b, 4c		emphasise the heading.

PRODUCING ENVIRONMENTAL COMPOST

Many people have decided that they should be doing something more useful with those banana skins, egg shells and other leftovers rather than just tipping them away into a bin. This also applies to garden rubbish – hedge trimmings, fallen leaves and weeds.

If you decide that you want to produce your own compost by using household waste you should be aware that you can follow some simple rules.

For the best results try to balance the contents of your bin. Aim for the ideal mixture. Two parts nitrogen-rich material, such as kitchen rubbish and grass clippings, to one part carbon-rich material, such as fallen leaves, straw or paper, Is Ideal. Too much of the former and the mixture will start to produce unpleasant odours, whereas too much of the latter will not allow it to rot down efficiently.

As a nation we are running out of places to put our waste. That is why we will have to reduce biodegradable rubbish going to landfill. More than half the nation's gardeners leave their debris out for the dustman. Local authorities are also starting to introduce compost collection schemes.

5b	3	Check through your work thoroughly and correct any errors you may have made. Save your document.
5d	4	Print a copy of your document.

What You Have To Do

Assessment Objectives		
2b	5	Insert the new paragraph below after the first paragraph. **With very little time and effort you can convert your household and garden waste into nutrient-rich compost for your flowerbeds and vegetable patch. Environmental organisations estimate that around 40% of all domestic refuse is compostable.**
2d	6	In the fourth paragraph beginning **... For the best results try to ...** delete the sentence **... Aim for the ideal mixture**.
4b	7	Insert a paragraph break and clear line space in the paragraph beginning **... For the best results try to ...** after the words **... straw or paper is ideal**.
2e	8	The word **rubbish** appears three times. Replace the word **rubbish** with the word **waste** each time it appears.
2c	9	Move the sentence shown below which appears in the final paragraph so that it becomes the last sentence in the first paragraph. **More than half the nation's gardeners leave their debris out for the dustman.**
3d, 5c, 5d	10	Fully justify the whole document except the heading. Save your file using a new filename. Print a copy of your document.
4a	11	Set in the whole document by 2 cm at both the right-hand and left-hand margins.
4c, 5d	12	Set the second paragraph *only* in double-line spacing. Print the document.
1a, 5e	13	Close down the word processing application in the correct sequence, making sure that the data is secure.

Self-assessment: Task 5

Did I do it correctly?

- [ ] Started up the word processing system
- [ ] Created a new document
- [ ] Entered the text in paragraphs
- [ ] Inserted text as specified
- [ ] Deleted text as specified
- [ ] Moved text as specified
- [ ] Replaced text as specified
- [ ] Used specified font and font size
- [ ] Changed the right-hand and left-hand margin widths as specified
- [ ] Changed the line spacing as specified
- [ ] Controlled the justification as specified
- [ ] Emphasised the specified text
- [ ] Saved the text
- [ ] Saved the text with a new filename
- [ ] Printed the document
- [ ] Closed documents.

UNIT 3 Electronic Communication Overview

What is electronic communication software?

This is a package that allows you to connect with a network of computers, people and information all over the world to (for example):

- exchange mail
- search for and locate an unlimited amount of information
- research projects
- keep up to date with world events through news bulletins
- conduct sales and purchases
- engage in leisure activities
- print the data you use and locate for further use.

Why use electronic communication software?

Using electronic communication software allows you to communicate with people all around the world. Through the e-mail facility you can send messages to and receive messages from business colleagues at your own site, or at other branches nationally and internationally, or to and from friends and family around the world. You can forward these messages to other people and groups to share the information.

You can also add further information to your message – eg text files, graphs, pictures and photographs – in the form of 'attachments'.

You can store e-mail addresses (in an address book so that it can be recalled and used without the need to re-key the data). Mail and attachments can be printed.

There will be facilities to allow you to 'surf' the World Wide Web using automatic links called 'hyperlinks' to move to other sites or pages.

The software will also enable you to use search engines to carry out site-specific (local) searches and general web searches to locate sites and pages to gather data or information or maybe to buy goods or services.

The software will allow you to store web addresses, save and print data from web pages.

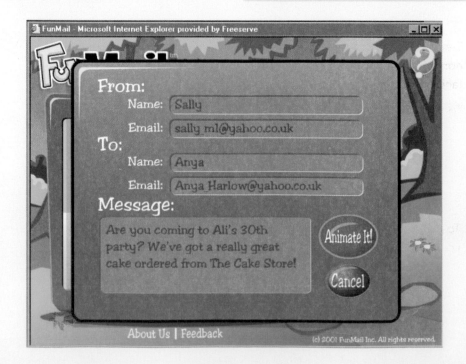

Input

This can be directly via the keyboard, or text can be prepared off-line. Data prepared off-line can be loaded more quickly and transmission costs minimised.

On-line/Off-line

When your computer is connected to the communication system and is ready for use, or not.

Processing

Data is transmitted from one computer to another via communication lines. To transfer the data you need communications software and a modem.

Output

You can print your mail and any attachments. Electronic messaging always identifies the sender, and usually gives the date and time the message was sent.

If you want to print data from the Internet you can either make a paper or 'hard' copy directly from the Web, or download the data and print later. Text usually prints quickly. Images may take some considerable time – if you do not need them, remove them before printing.

Electronic communication actions

Electronic communications software will normally allow you to use **e-mail** and **Internet** facilities.

To create and send e-mail messages you must enter the details of the person to whom the message is directed, and your message. If you do not enter the address correctly the message will not reach the destination and the system will normally inform you.

To add or attach documents to your e-mails you must specify the file names. These are often condensed (or zipped) for speed of transmission. You may need to unzip the files before use.

On receipt of an e-mail you will be given details including the Subject or title and the Sender. Be careful when opening e-mail as this is a way of spreading a virus. Your system will normally issue warnings regarding opening mail and attachments.

When you have received e-mail you can use that message to reply and you can also forward the e-mail to another person or group of people. You should also be able to add e-mail addresses to an address book so that you do not have to re-enter the details each time you send mail to that person.

You will also have the facility to delete e-mail and e-mail attachments.

You will be able to store your e-mails, and any attachments, to keep data from a web page and both e-mail and web addresses (URL).

Electronic communication terms

Log on/Log off

The procedure for starting the system so that you can use it, and the correct sequence in which to close the system down when you have completed the session. Use of the system should be controlled by a password.

Modem

An abbreviation for modulator-demodulator. It is a device for converting a **digital** signal generated by a computer into an **analogue** signal. In this form the signal can be transmitted along a telephone line.

Hyperlinks

Most web sites include hyperlinks. A hyperlink is a way of getting from one page to another destination without having to enter the address. You may also move to a different location on the same page (a picture, an e-mail address or a program).

Search engines

These are programs that enable you to search the Internet by keywords or topics.

33

HTML

Hypertext markup language describes the contents and appearance of elements on a page, such as paragraph, table, or image.

GIF files

Images that can add a dynamic element, promote specific information and events and highlight navigation.

URL

To get to a site you enter an Internet address in the space provided on the browser. Web addresses, sometimes called uniform resource locators (URLs), begin with http:// – hypertext transfer protocol.

Navigation

After you enter the web address, the site's homepage will appear. You will then have more choices to take you further into the site.

Attachments

An attachment is any file that is added to an e-mail message. It may be a text file, image, photograph, etc. You can send and receive attachments. They can be stored with the e-mail or saved separately.

Bookmarks

A bookmark is a location or selected text on a page that you have marked so that you can return to it.

Helping you pass

Critical errors

- An incorrect or omitted e-mail address.
- A missing or incorrect attachment.
- Failing to locate and print specified web pages.

Accuracy errors

- Check the data you have entered as each **missing, incorrect or extra word** will count as a separate accuracy error. **Note**: A mistake in the subject heading will count as one accuracy error only.
- Check that you have completed all the objectives as each one not met will count as a separate error.

Tips

- When you **create the new message** it must not contain RE: or FW: in the subject heading and you should not include any quoted text from a previous message.

Introduction to Tasks 1 to 3

In Tasks 1 to 3 you will have to access an e-mail message, an image file, and the Internet.

You will find the image **cologo.gif** on the CD supplied with this book.

To carry out Tasks 1–3 your tutor will need to make the following available to you before you begin:

1   The e-mail message, with capitalisation as shown, to send to you:

Subject:	New logo
Message:	I have attached the new college logo. It should be used immediately.
Signature:	Course Planning Manager
Attachment:	cologo.gif

This e-mail will be accessed at step 1 of Task 1. The attachment will be used at steps 1, 2 and 4.

2   An e-mail address from which this message will be sent and to which you will send a reply. The address will also be stored in an address book, and a new message will be sent to it. The address (or its nickname/alias) must be identical on each of these occasions.

3   Two further e-mail addresses. OCR supplies two dummy addresses for use. E-mail sent to these addresses is not read or assessed in any way.
OCR dummy addresses:
admin@progress-media.co.uk
manager@progress-media.co.uk

If you are unable to use these addresses, suitable equivalents may be substituted. They should be clearly identifiable as **admin** and **manager**, ie these names should form part of the addresses.

If you use alternatives, then insert the alternative e-mail addresses for **admin** and **manager** at step 2 of Task 1, and step 2 of Task 2. These addresses *must* be reflected in the work.

4   Before starting the task, and to enable evidence of the storage of the specified address, ensure that the address storage facility has been entirely cleared (step 1 of Task 1).

5   Access to the Progress Media web site is required (step 1 of Task 2). This web site is available at a number of addresses (mirrors). A list of current mirrors is maintained on the main web site at the URL:
www.progress-media.co.uk/status.htm

At the time of publication, the following mirrors are available:
www.progress-mirror1.co.uk
www.progress-mirror2.co.uk

6   You should note the addresses of the mirror sites in advance. If difficulty is experienced in accessing the Progress Media web site using the URLs provided, the alternative server addresses may be used. Please note that only the server address (everything preceding the '/') needs to be substituted.

7   The application's bookmark facility should be cleared, and any 'history' and 'auto-completion' facilities of the browsing software should be disabled. The bookmark facility should also be cleared following completion of the tasks.

Build Up Exercises

TASK 1

This task is designed to allow you to practise the skills required to gain OCR Level 1 Certificate for IT Users (NEW CLAIT) assessment objectives.

Before you begin

You will need to find out and note down how to:

- load appropriate software to use e-mail and browsing facilities
- access an incoming message
- forward a message
- reply to a message
- access an attached file
- store an e-mail address
- delete an e-mail message
- store an e-mail attachment
- print messages and attachments.

There is a checklist for you to complete on page 39 to use as a reference sheet.

Scenario

You are working as an administrator for a college. The college has recently amalgamated with two others in the area. Your duties include:

- acting as the e-mail distributor
- locating and producing data from college resources
- locating and producing data from the Internet.

Assessment Objectives		What You Have To Do
		The Course Planning Manager has sent you an e-mail message containing a copy of the new logo for the college.
1a, 2b, 2f 5c, 5e	1	Open your mailbox and read the message entitled **New logo** from the Course Planning Manager.
		Add the sender's e-mail address to your address book.
		Print a copy of the attached file, **cologo.gif**.
2d	2	You must inform the Administration Department. Prepare to forward the message **New logo** and its attachment to **admin@progress-media.co.uk** adding the following text:
		The new logo is attached.
		Add your name and centre number to the end of the message.
		Check your message for errors and, making sure that your system saves outgoing messages, forward the e-mail message including the attachment.

What You Have To Do

Assessment Objectives		
2c	3	You should also let the Course Planning Manager know that you have received the design. Prepare a reply to the Course Planning Manager using the following message: **Thank you for the logo. I have forwarded it to the Administration Department.** Add your name and centre number to the end of the message. Check your message for errors and, making sure that your system saves outgoing messages, send the reply.
5b, 5d	4	You have to manage your mailbox to reduce storage demands. Save the attachment **cologo.gif** separately from the mailbox and delete the message entitled **New logo**.

TASK 2

This task is designed to allow you to practise the skills required to gain OCR Level 1 Certificate for IT Users (NEW CLAIT) assessment objectives.

Before you begin

You will need to find out and note down how to:

- create a new message and copy a message
- attach a file to an e-mail message
- access specified web pages
- navigate the Word Wide Web using hyperlinks
- use a site-specific (local) search engine
- save data from a web page
- store a web address (URL).

What You Have To Do

Assessment Objectives		
3a, 3b, 4a 4d, 5a, 5f	I	In order to plan possible course places the Course Planning Manager needs data on average population growth in a medium size city. A graph showing this data is one of the many that can be found on the college's web site. Access the college's web site at: **www.progress-media.co.uk** Follow the links to the Search page. Use the local search facility to locate a page on the site displaying a graph of **population growth in a medium city**. Bookmark the page and print one copy. Save the graph as **popgrow.gif**.

What You Have To Do

Assessment Objectives		
2a, 2e, 2g	2	Prepare a new e-mail message to the Course Planning Manager using the e-mail address recalled from your address book. The subject heading should be: **CITY POPULATION** Use the following message: **Please find attached the graph showing population growth in a medium city.** Locate and attach the file **popgrow.gif** saved at step 1. Add your name and centre number to the end of the message. Make sure that a copy of your message is sent to your manager at: **manager@progress-media.co.uk** Check your message for errors and, making sure that your system saves outgoing messages, send the message and attachment.

TASK 3

This task is designed to allow you to practise the skills required to gain OCR Level 1 Certificate for IT Users (NEW CLAIT) assessment objectives.

Before you begin

You will need to find out and note down how to:

- use a general web search engine
- locate web pages containing required data
- print web pages.

What You Have To Do

Assessment Objectives		
4b, 4c 5a, 5f	1	The Course Planning Manager would also like to carry out some further research including population estimates. Use a web-based search engine to search for web pages containing official figures for the UK population. Follow links to find a specific web page containing any new research projects showing: **small area population estimates.** Bookmark the page and print one copy.
5e	2	Locate the copies of the messages you have sent and print a copy of each message. Make sure that header details (To, From, Date and Subject) are shown. Make sure that attachments are indicated where appropriate.
5a	3	Access the bookmark facility and ask your tutor to check the stored bookmarks.
la	4	Exit the software securely.

Electronic Communication Checklist

You should complete this checklist for each hardware and software combination you use. Use information from your tutor, handouts, handbooks and software manuals to complete the list. You can then use your list as a reference sheet to complete the practice tasks that follow.

Hardware: _____

Software: _____

ASSESSMENT OBJECTIVE	HOW TO DO IT	OCR REFERENCE
1 Identify and use e-mail and browsing software		
Use appropriate application software	_____	la
2 Transmit and receive e-mail messages and attachments		
Create a new message	_____	2a
Access incoming message	_____	2b
Reply to message	_____	2c
Forward message	_____	2d
Copy message	_____	2e
Access attached file	_____	2f
Attach file to e-mail message	_____	2g
Recall stored e-mail address	_____	2h
3 Navigate the World Wide Web		
Access specified web page(s)	_____	3a
Navigate the World Wide Web using hyperlinks	_____	3b
4 Use search techniques to locate data on the Web		
Use a site-specific (local) search engine	_____	4a
Use a general web search engine	_____	4b
Locate web page(s) containing required data	_____	4c
Save data from web page	_____	4d
5 Manage and print electronic documents		
Store web address (URL)	_____	5a
Delete e-mail message	_____	5b
Store e-mail address	_____	5c
Store e-mail attachment	_____	5d
Print message(s) and attachment	_____	5e
Print web page(s)	_____	5f

OCR Assignments and Self-Assessments

TASK **4**

This task allows you to practise a complete OCR Level 1 Certificate for IT Users (NEW CLAIT) assignment. It covers all the OCR Level 1 Certificate for IT Users (NEW CLAIT) electronic communication assessment objectives.

In this task you will have to access an e-mail message, an image file, and the Internet.

 You will find the image **dragon.gif** on the CD supplied with this book.

To carry out this task your tutor will need to make the following available to you:

1   The e-mail message, with capitalisation as shown, to send to you:

Subject:	Dragon Design
Message:	This design is now ready for production
Signature:	Design Department
Attachment:	dragon.gif

This e-mail will be accessed at step 1. The attachment will be used at steps 1, 2 and 4.

2   An e-mail address from which this message will be sent, and to which you will send a reply. The address will also be stored in an address book, and a new message will be sent to it. The address (or its nickname/alias) must be identical on each of these occasions.

3   Two further e-mail addresses. OCR supplies two dummy addresses for use. E-mail sent to these addresses is not read or assessed in any way.
OCR dummy addresses:
admin@progress-media.co.uk
manager@progress-media.co.uk

If you are unable to use these addresses, suitable equivalents may be substituted. They should be clearly identifiable as **admin** and **manager**, ie these names should form part of the addresses.

If you use alternatives then insert the alternative e-mail addresses for **admin** and **manager** at step 2 and step 7. These addresses *must* be reflected in the work.

4   Before starting the task, to enable evidence of the storage of the specified address, ensure that the address storage facility has been entirely cleared (step 1).

5   Access to the Progress Media web site is required (step 5). This web site is available at a number of addresses (mirrors). A list of current mirrors is maintained on the main web site at the URL:
www.progress-media.co.uk/status.htm

At the time of publication, the following mirrors are available:
www.progress-mirror1.co.uk
www.progress-mirror2.co.uk

6   You should note the addresses of the mirror sites in advance. If difficulty is experienced in accessing the Progress Media web site using the URLs provided, the alternative server addresses may be used. Please note that only the server address (everything preceding the '/') needs to be substituted.

7   The application's bookmark facility should be cleared, and any 'history' and 'auto-completion' facilities of the browsing software should be disabled. The bookmark facility should also be cleared following completion of the tasks.

Scenario

You are working as an administrator for Progress Kites. Your duties include:

- acting as the e-mail distributor for the company
- locating and producing data from the company's resources
- locating and producing data from the Internet.

		What You Have To Do
Assessment Objectives		**The Design Department Manager has sent you an e-mail message containing a copy of the design for a new kite that is about to go into production.**
la, 2b, 2f 5c, 5e	l	Open your mailbox and read the message entitled **Dragon Design** from the Design Department Manager.
		Add the sender's e-mail address to your address book.
		Print a copy of the attached file, **dragon.gif**.
2d	2	You must inform the Production and Administration Department Manager that the design is now ready for production. Prepare to forward the message **Dragon Design** and its attachment to **admin@progress-media.co.uk** adding the following text: **Please find attached the design for the new kite.**
		Add your name and centre number to the end of your message.
		Check your message for errors and, making sure that your system saves outgoing messages, forward the e-mail message including the attachment.
2c	3	You should also let the Design Department Manager know that you have received the design. Prepare a reply to the Design Department Manager using the following message: **Thank you for the design. I have forwarded it to the Production and Administration Department Manager.**
		Add your name and centre number to the end of the message.
		Check your message for errors and, making sure that your system saves outgoing messages, send the reply.

What You Have To Do

Assessment Objectives		
5b, 5d	4	You have to manage your mailbox to reduce storage demands. Save the attachment **dragon.gif** separately from the mailbox and delete the message entitled **Dragon Design**.
3a, 3b, 4a 4d, 5a	5	The Design Department Manager needs data on kite costs. A graph showing this data is one of the many that can be found on the company's web site.
		Access the company's web site at: **www.progress-media.co.uk**
		Follow the links to the Search page. Use the local search facility to locate a page on the site displaying a graph of **kite sizes and costs**.
		Bookmark the page and print one copy.
		Save the graph as **kcosts.gif**.
4b, 4c 5a, 5f	6	You have received a number of enquiries from customers about clubs in their area that they can join.
		Use a web-based search engine to search for web pages containing data on clubs, teams and people involved in this activity in the UK. Follow links to find a specific web page showing: **UK kite clubs, teams and people.**
		Bookmark the page and print one copy.
2a, 2e, 2g 2h	7	Prepare a new e-mail message to the Design Department Manager using the e-mail address recalled from your address book.
		The subject heading should be: **Kite Sizes and Costs**
		Use the following message: **Please find attached the graph showing kite sizes and costs.**
		Locate and attach the file **kcosts.gif** saved at step 5.
		Add your name and centre number to the end of the message.
		Make sure that a copy of your message will be sent to your manager at: <u>manager@progress-media.co.uk</u>
		Check your message for errors and, making sure that your system saves outgoing messages, send the message and attachment.
5e	8	Locate the copies of the messages you have sent and print a copy of each message. Make sure that header details (To, From, Date and Subject) are shown. Make sure that attachments are indicated where appropriate.
5a	9	Access the bookmark facility and ask your tutor to check the stored bookmarks.
1a	10	Exit the software securely.

Self-assessment: Task 4

Did I do it correctly?

☐ Used appropriate application software

☐ Accessed the incoming message entitled **Dragon Design** with the attached file **dragon.gif**

☐ Stored the sender's e-mail address in your address book

☐ Forwarded the message **Dragon Design** and its attachment to **admin@progress-media.co.uk**

☐ Replied to the e-mail **Dragon Design**

☐ Deleted the e-mail message **Dragon Design**

☐ Accessed the company's website at: **www.progress-media.co.uk**

☐ Used local search facilities to locate a web page displaying a graph of **kite sizes and costs**

☐ Navigated the World Wide Web using hyperlinks

☐ Used a web-based search engine to search for web pages showing **UK Kite clubs, teams and people**

☐ Prepared a new e-mail message to the Design Department Manager using:
- the e-mail address recalled from your address book
- the subject heading: **Kite Sizes and Costs**
- the message: **Please find attached the graph showing kite costs and sizes** and put your name and centre number to the end of the message
- the attachment **kcosts.gif**

☐ Sent a copy of the message **Kite Sizes and Costs**, to your manager at: **manager@progress-media.co.uk**

☐ Stored the:
- e-mail attachment **dragon.gif**
- web page displaying **kite sizes and costs** as **kcosts.gif**

☐ Printed:
- each message that you sent
- the attachment **dragon.gif**
- the web page showing a graph of **kite sizes and costs**
- the web page showing **UK Kite clubs, teams and people**

☐ Placed a bookmark on the web page showing:
- a graph of **kite sizes and costs**
- **UK Kite clubs, teams and people**

TASK 5

This task allows you to practise a complete OCR Level 1 Certificate for IT Users (NEW CLAIT) assignment. It covers all the OCR Level 1 Certificate for IT Users (NEW CLAIT) electronic communication assessment objectives.

In this task you will have to access an e-mail message, an image file, and the Internet.

You will find the image **birds.gif** on the CD that is supplied with this book.

To carry out this task your tutor will need to make the following available to you:

1   The e-mail message, with capitalisation as shown, to send to you:

Subject:	**Bird Fabric**
Message:	**I am happy to proceed with the project using this design, into which I have incorporated a few colour amendments.**
Signature:	**Morton Interiors**
Attachment:	**birds.gif**

This e-mail will be accessed at step 1. The attachment will be used at steps 1, 2 and 4.

2   An e-mail address from which this message will be sent, and to which you will send a reply. The address will also be stored in an address book, and a new message will be sent to it. The address (or its nickname/alias) must be identical on each of these occasions.

3   Two further e-mail addresses. OCR supplies two dummy addresses for use. E-mail sent to these addresses is not read or assessed in any way.

OCR dummy addresses:
admin@progress-media.co.uk
manager@progress-media.co.uk

If you are unable to use these addresses, suitable equivalents may be substituted. They should be clearly identifiable as **admin** and **manager**, ie these names should form part of the addresses.

If you use alternatives then insert the alternative e-mail addresses for **admin** and **manager** at step 2 and step 7. These addresses *must* be reflected in the work.

4   Before starting the task, to enable evidence of the storage of the specified address, ensure that the address storage facility has been entirely cleared (step 1).

5   Access to the Progress Media web site is required (step 5). This web site is available at a number of addresses (mirrors). A list of current mirrors is maintained on the main web site at the URL:
www.progress-media.co.uk/status.htm

At the time of publication, the following mirrors are available:
www.progress-mirror1.co.uk
www.progress-mirror2.co.uk

6 You should note the addresses of the mirror sites in advance. If difficulty is experienced in accessing the Progress Media web site using the URLs provided, the alternative server addresses may be used. Please note that only the server address (everything preceding the '/') needs to be substituted.

7 The application's bookmark facility should be cleared, and any 'history' and 'auto-completion' facilities of the browsing software should be disabled. The bookmark facility should also be cleared following completion of the tasks.

Scenario

You are working as an administrator for Progress Media Ltd, a graphic design company. Your duties include:

- acting as the e-mail distributor for the company between the freelance designers and clients
- locating and producing data from your company's resources
- locating and producing data from the Internet.

What You Have To Do		
Assessment Objectives		**One of the clients has sent you an e-mail message containing a copy of their new design.**
la, 2b, 2f 5c, 5e	I	Open your mailbox and read the message entitled **Bird Fabric** from the client.
		Add the sender's e-mail address to your address book.
		Print a copy of the attached file, **birds.gif**.
2d	2	You must inform the designer that the client has accepted the design. Prepare to forward the message **Bird Fabric** and its attachment to **admin@progress-media.co.uk** adding the following text: **This design for Morton Interiors can now proceed to the next phase of the project.**
		Add your name and centre number to the end of your message.
		Check your message for errors and, making sure that your system saves outgoing messages, forward the e-mail message including the attachment.
2c	3	You should also let the client know that you have received the design. Prepare a reply to the client using the following message: **Thank you for design approval. I have forwarded your changes to your designer.**
		Add your name and centre number to the end of the message.
		Check your message for errors and, making sure that your system saves outgoing messages, send the reply.

What You Have To Do

Assessment Objectives		
5b, 5d	4	You have to manage your mailbox to reduce storage demands. Save the attachment **birds.gif** separately from the mailbox and delete the message entitled **Bird Fabric**.
3a, 3b, 4a 4d, 5a	5	The client is concerned about the costs of the project, and has asked for information regarding the fees for the graphic designers. A graph of this data is one of the many that can be found on the company's web site.
		Access the company's web site at:
		www.progress-media.co.uk
		Follow the links to the Search page. Use the local search facility to locate a page on the site displaying a graph of **Consultancy Rates for Graphic Designers**.
		Bookmark the page and print one copy.
		Save the graph as **gdrates.gif**.
4b, 4c 5a, 5f	6	In order to ensure that you are paying your designers at the 'market rate' you will need to identify the fees for graphic designers in the open market.
		Use a web-based search engine to search for web pages containing **UK contractor rates**. Follow links to find a specific web page showing **market data** on **highest earning skills**.
		Bookmark the page and print one copy.
2a, 2e, 2g	7	Prepare a new e-mail message to the client using the e-mail address recalled from your address book.
		The subject heading should be: **Design Costs**
		Use the following message: **Please find attached the graph showing the consultancy rates for our graphic designers.**
		Locate and attach the file **gdrates.gif** saved at step 5.
		Add your name and centre number to the end of the message.
		Make sure that a copy of your message will be sent to your manager at: **manager@progress-media.co.uk**
		Check your message for errors and, making sure that your system saves outgoing messages, send the message and attachment.
5e	8	Locate the copies of the messages you have sent and print a copy of each message. Make sure that header details (To, From, Date and Subject) are shown. Make sure that attachments are indicated where appropriate.
5a	9	Access the bookmark facility and ask your tutor to check the stored bookmarks.
1a	10	Exit the software securely.

Self-assessment: Task 5

Did I do it correctly?

- ☐ Used appropriate application software
- ☐ Created a new message
- ☐ Accessed incoming message
- ☐ Replied to a message
- ☐ Forwarded a message
- ☐ Copied a message
- ☐ Accessed an attached file
- ☐ Attached a file to an e-mail message
- ☐ Recalled a stored e-mail address
- ☐ Accessed specified web page(s)
- ☐ Navigated the World Wide Web using hyperlinks
- ☐ Used a site-specific (local) search engine
- ☐ Used a general web search engine
- ☐ Located web page(s) containing required data
- ☐ Saved data from a web page
- ☐ Stored a web address (URL)
- ☐ Deleted an e-mail message
- ☐ Stored an e-mail address
- ☐ Stored an e-mail attachment
- ☐ Printed a message and an attachment
- ☐ Printed web page(s).

UNIT 4 — Spreadsheets Overview

What is a spreadsheet?

A spreadsheet allows you to enter and store data in a 'grid' format on a computer system. It will provide you with a means of performing numerical and statistical calculations.

Why use a spreadsheet?

With a spreadsheet, once you have entered the appropriate formulae, the program will perform the necessary calculation. Any of the entries can be changed, including numeric data and formulae. The effects these changes have on the results of the calculations will be displayed automatically. You will not have to recalculate the figures yourself. Spreadsheets can be used to present a wide variety of information such as budgets, petty cash records, weather information, etc. The data can be stored on disk and printed out when required.

Contents

Numeric data

When numbers are entered in a spreadsheet they can form the basis of any calculation you require.

Text

You can enter words into cells on your spreadsheet. This will provide important information to help you and others understand the numeric entries on the spreadsheet. Text will be used for titles, headings and any notes. Text entries can include numbers if they are not required for calculation purposes.

Formulae functions

Formulae are the instructions to the system to perform calculations. They will allow you to multiply, divide, add and subtract any numbers on your spreadsheet.

Formula

Column

Row

Cell

Microsoft Excel - DEC-FIGURES.xls

File Edit View Insert Format Tools Data Window Help Acrobat

SUM   =SUM(E4:E10)

	A	B	C	D	E	F	G	H
1	**December**	**Figures**						
2	**Code**	**Description**	**Cost**	**No. Sold**	**Revenue**			
3	**Wedding Cakes**							
4	WD-02	Standard two-tier	£ 90.00	1	£ 90.00			
5	WD-03	Standard three-tier	£ 120.00	2	£ 240.00			
6	WD-04	Standard four-tier	£ 150.00	0	£ -			
7	WD-05	Standard five-tier	£ 200.00	1	£ 200.00			
8	WD-06	Personalised level 1	£ 250.00	0	£ -			
9	WD-07	Personalised level 2	£ 300.00	1	£ 300.00			
10	WD-08	Personalised level 3	£ 350.00	0	£			
11	CATEGORY TOTAL			5	=SUM(E4:E10)			
12								
13	**Birthday Cakes**							
14	BT-01	Roses	£ 20.00	0	£ -			
15	BT-02	Train	£ 30.00	1	£ 30.00			
16	BT-03	Teddy	£ 30.00	2	£ 60.00			
17	BT-04	Pony	£ 30.00	1	£ 30.00			
18	BT-05	Wizard	£ 40.00	5	£ 200.00			
19	BT-06	Cat	£ 30.00	2	£ 60.00			
20	BT-07	Dog	£ 30.00	1	£ 30.00			
21	BT-08	Personalised level 1	£ 40.00	0	£ -			
22	BT-09	Personalised level 2	£ 50.00	2	£ 100.00			
23	BT-10	Personalised level 3	£ 60.00	1	£ 60.00			
24	CATEGORY TOTAL			15	£ 480.00			
25								
26	**Anniversary Cakes**							
27	AN-01	Silver	£ 30.00	1	£ 30.00			
28	AN-02	Golden	£ 30.00	0	£ -			
29	AN-03	Ruby	£ 30.00	1	£ 30.00			
30	AN-04	Personalised level 1	£ 40.00	1	£ 40.00			
31	AN-05	Personalised level 2	£ 50.00	0	£ -			
32	AN-06	Personalised level 3	£ 60.00	0	£ -			

Sheet1 / Sheet2 / Sheet3

Draw - AutoShapes -

Edit

Start   Explorin... | Paint S... | Inbox - | Yahoo!... | CLIENT...

When keying in the formulae you use the

+   for addition
-   for subtraction
*   is normally used for multiplication, and
/   is normally used for division.

The spreadsheet package will also recognise cell references and signs such as > (greater than) and < (less than).

Functions are instructions to the system to carry out a particular process. Each function has a word the system recognises, eg SUM(B1...B5) will add all the numeric values stored in cells B1, B2, B3, B4 and B5.

Structure

Row

This is a line of cells across the spreadsheet. Each row has a reference letter or number.

Column

This is a line of cells down the spreadsheet. Each column is normally referenced by a letter.

Cell

A single 'box' on the spreadsheet grid is called a cell.

Cell references

Each cell can be identified by giving its row and column reference.

Layout

Spreadsheet display

This is the view of the spreadsheet on the screen.

Scrolling

A complete spreadsheet may well be too large for all of it to be shown at one time on the screen. You can scroll to the left and right or up and down until the part of the spreadsheet you want to see is visible.

Status area

This area on the screen display gives information about the particular spreadsheet you are working on. The information it contains will vary from program to program. The information normally includes the contents of the cell currently being used, the name of the spreadsheet file and the storage space remaining on the computer.

Command line

This area on the screen display is usually just below the spreadsheet display. The command line shows your entry or command being entered in the current cell before the enter or return key is pressed.

Display

When selecting the display for data on a spreadsheet you can choose the layout for each cell or for a range of cells, such as a row or column or part of a row or column.

Text

Text can be displayed left-aligned, right-aligned or centred.

Numeric data

There are several ways in which numeric data can be displayed. You should be able to choose:

- how many decimal places to display
- to display in pounds and pence (ie with two decimal places)
- to display data in integer format (ie rounding to the nearest whole number)
- to align your display to the right or to the left, although remember it is more common to align numbers to the right.

Column width

Spreadsheet packages will allow you to control the width of individual columns. It may be necessary to adjust the width of a column to show all the information.

Features

Editing

The editing facility allows you to change figures, text or formulae on a spreadsheet. You may need to correct a mistake made when entering the data, or perhaps the circumstances have changed and the data needs to be revised.

Your package should allow you to insert a new row or column or to delete a row or column you no longer require.

Replicating

The replicating facility allows you to copy the contents of one cell to another cell or range of cells. This can be very useful if, for example, the same formula has to be entered at the same point (in every column). You enter the formula once and then replicate it down the whole column. The spreadsheet will automatically 'advance' the formula.

Copy

The copy facility allows you to copy the contents of one cell or a range of cells from one part of the spreadsheet to another. This can be very useful if, for example, the same figure has to be entered at the same point (in every column). You simply enter the figure once and then copy it down the whole column or row.

Generating new values

A major advantage of using a spreadsheet is that it quickly recalculates the effects of changes to any of the entries. This is often referred to as the 'what if' facility. For example, WHAT would happen to the price of these goods IF there was an increase of 15% in the wage costs?

Printing

The data stored by your spreadsheet can be printed in two ways:

- the actual entries on the spreadsheet – ie the figures
- the formulae entered to produce the results.

You should be able to choose whether to print the whole spreadsheet or only part of it.

Need for accuracy

You should always enter numeric data very carefully. Incorrect entries on a spreadsheet will make the results of the spreadsheet inaccurate.

Helping you pass

Critical errors

- Failing to generate and display correct results.
- Failing to delete/insert specified row/column.

Accuracy errors

- Check the data you have entered **as any errors within a cell** containing a label will count as a separate accuracy error. **Note** that if numeric data is not 100% accurate this counts as a critical error.
- Check that you have completed all the objectives as each one not met will count as a separate error.

Tips

- Check that all the columns are wide enough to display **all** the data.
- When you replicate (copy) do not leave formulae in blank rows or columns.

Build Up Exercises

TASK 1

This task is designed to allow you to practise the skills required to gain OCR Level 1 Certificate for IT Users (NEW CLAIT) assessment objectives.

Before you begin

You will need to find out and note down how to:

- switch on your system
- load your spreadsheet application
- create a new spreadsheet
- enter text and numeric data
- save your spreadsheet
- print spreadsheet data in full.

There is a checklist for you to complete on page 54 to use as a reference sheet.

Scenario

You work as an administrative assistant for Progress Holidays. You are responsible for a variety of tasks, including production of routine financial reports.

What You Have To Do

Assessment Objectives		
Ia, 5a	I	**Your manager has asked you to produce a spreadsheet showing the number of holidays sold to countries in Europe and the Americas.** Load your spreadsheet application and create a new spreadsheet.
2a	2	Enter the following data, leaving the **INCOME** column blank.

DESTINATION	JULY	AUG	SEPT	OCT	COST	TAXES	INCOME
AMERICA	1236	2985	2919	1562	1125.5	35	
AUSTRALIA	3922	2905	2584	4000	2269.55	45	
AUSTRIA	5682	4356	3287	2176	569.55	18.5	
CARRIBEAN	3465	4365	3244	2984	1585.6	30	
FRANCE	8703	3249	2219	4790	850.65	18.5	
GERMANY	4254	3502	2298	2135	950.55	18.5	
IRELAND	7234	1974	3878	1365	550.05	15.5	
ITALY	1765	9875	3830	1827	755.45	18.5	
SPAIN	4545	3444	3568	4367	650	18.5	

2a	3	Enter your name, centre number and today's date below the data.
5b, 5e	4	Save the spreadsheet and print one copy, showing the figures not the formulae. Ensure that all the data is displayed in full.

This task is designed to allow you to practise the skills required to gain OCR Level 1 Certificate for IT Users (NEW CLAIT) assessment objectives.

Before you begin

You will need to find out and note down how to:

- change entries made to your spreadsheet
- insert row/column
- delete row/column
- recalculate data
- enter formulae
- replicate formulae (fill)
- save your spreadsheet using a new filename
- print spreadsheet data in full.

What You Have To Do

Assessment Objectives		
2b	I	Using the file from Task 1, insert a new column entitled **TOTAL SALES** between the columns **OCT** and **COST**.
3a, 3b	2	The **TOTAL SALES** figure is the sum of the figures for the months **JULY** to **OCT**.
		Insert a formula to calculate the **TOTAL SALES** for **AMERICA**.
		Replicate this formula to show the **TOTAL SALES** for each of the other destinations.
3a, 3b	3	**INCOME** is calculated by adding the **COST** and **TAXES** and then multiplying by the **TOTAL SALES**.
		Insert a formula to calculate the **INCOME** for **AMERICA**.
		Replicate this formula to show the **INCOME** for each of the other destinations.
2d, 3c	4	Your manager has identified a few errors in the original data. Make the following amendments, and ensure that the **INCOME** figures are updated as a result of these changes.
		a The **SEPT** figure for **AMERICA** should be **2999**
		b **CARIBBEAN** is incorrect, please correct it
		c The **COST** for **FRANCE** should be **855.65**
		d The **AUG** figure for **SPAIN** should be **4344**
2c	5	The **AUSTRALIA** figures should be in the Australasian group. Delete the entire row for **AUSTRALIA**.
5c, 5e	6	Save the spreadsheet with a new filename and print the spreadsheet showing values not formulae. Ensure that all the data is displayed in full.

TASK 3

This task is designed to allow you to practise the skills required to gain OCR Level 1 Certificate for IT Users (NEW CLAIT) assessment objectives.

Before you begin

You will need to find out and note down how to:

- left and right align text and numerical data
- use integer format to display numbers (to 0 decimal places)
- use decimal format to display numbers (to 2 decimal places)
- use currency format to display numbers (to include £ sign)
- print with formulae showing in full
- close spreadsheet.

What You Have To Do

Assessment Objectives		What You Have To Do
4a, 4b	1	Apply alignment as follows: a The row labels (**DESTINATION** to **SPAIN**) should be left-aligned. b The column headings (**JULY** to **INCOME**) should be right-aligned. c All numeric data should be right-aligned.
4c, 4d, 4e	2	Format the data as follows: a All the figures from **JULY** to **OCT** and the **TOTAL SALES** figures should be displayed in integer format (0 decimal places). b The **COST** and **TAXES** figures should be displayed to 2 decimal places. c The **INCOME** figures should be displayed with a £ sign and to 2 decimal places.
5b, 5e	3	Save your file and print one copy showing the values (figures) not the formulae. Ensure that all the data is displayed in full.
5d	4	Print the spreadsheet with all formulae showing. Ensure that all the formulae are displayed in full.
1a, 5f	5	Close your spreadsheet and exit the software securely.

Spreadsheets Checklist

You should complete this checklist for each hardware and software combination you use. Use information from your tutor, handouts, handbooks and software manuals to complete the list. You can then use your list as a reference sheet to complete the practice tasks that follow.

Hardware: _____

Software: _____

ASSESSMENT OBJECTIVE	HOW TO DO IT	OCR REFERENCE
1 Identify and use spreadsheet software correctly		
Use appropriate application software	_____	1a
2 Use an input device to enter and edit data accurately		
Insert text and numerical data	_____	2a
Insert row/column	_____	2b
Delete row/column	_____	2c
Amend text and numerical data	_____	2d
3 Insert, replicate and format arithmetical formulae		
Insert formulae	_____	3a
Replicate formulae (fill)	_____	3b
Recalculate data	_____	3c
4 Use common numerical formatting and alignment		
Align text	_____	4a
Align numerical data	_____	4b
Display as integer (to 0 dec places)	_____	4c
Display as decimal (to 2 dec places)	_____	4d
Display as currency (to include £ sign)	_____	4e
5 Manage and print spreadsheet documents		
Create a new spreadsheet	_____	5a
Save spreadsheet	_____	5b
Save spreadsheet with new filename	_____	5c
Print with formulae showing in full	_____	5d
Print with data showing in full	_____	5e
Close spreadsheet	_____	5f

OCR Assignments and Self-Assessments

TASK 4

This task allows you to practise a complete OCR Level 1 Certificate for IT Users (NEW CLAIT) assignment. It covers all the OCR Level 1 Certificate for IT Users (NEW CLAIT) spreadsheets assessment objectives.

Scenario

You work as an administrative assistant for Progress NPS. You are responsible for a variety of tasks, including production of routine financial reports.

What You Have To Do

Assessment Objectives		
1a, 5a	1	**Your manager has asked you to produce a spreadsheet report showing product sales in UK countries.** Load your spreadsheet application and create a new spreadsheet.
2a	2	Enter the following data, leaving the **VAT** and **INCOME** columns blank.

ITEM CODE	SCOTLAND	IRELAND	ENGLAND	WALES	COST	VAT	INCOME
GB1681	31450	36425	45180	15871	13.95		
GB1682	48145	41120	39995	16587	19.4		
GB1683	22555	21267	28254	29850	24.99		
GH5679	23005	23297	25374	26802	29.9		
GH5680	11721	29129	14372	19850	45.5		
TY3090	13813	30126	22125	19835	49.55		
TY3091	27860	34820	23578	21530	50.25		
TY3093	48145	41120	39995	16587	49.4		
WP306	16549	73662	35276	45300	61.85		
WP307	47608	59700	21099	30466	75.6		

2a, 5b	3	Enter your name, centre number and today's date below the data and print one copy showing the figures. Ensure that all the data is shown in full.
2a, 2b	4	Insert a new column entitled **TOTAL** between the columns **WALES** and **COST**
3a, 3b	5	The **TOTAL** figure is the sum of the figures from **SCOTLAND** to **WALES**. Insert a formula to calculate the **TOTAL** for item code **GB1681**. Replicate this formula to show the **TOTAL** for each of the other item codes.

What You Have To Do

Assessment Objectives		
3a, 3b	6	**VAT** is 17.5% of the **COST** figure. Insert a formula to calculate the **VAT** for item code **GB1681**. Replicate this formula to show the **VAT** for each of the other item codes.
3a, 3b	7	**INCOME** is calculated by adding the **COST** and **VAT** and then multiplying by the **TOTAL**. Insert a formula to calculate the **INCOME** for item code **GB1681**. Replicate this formula to show the **INCOME** for each of the other item codes.
2c	8	The **IRELAND** figures should not be included in this group. Delete the entire column for **IRELAND**.
2d, 3c	9	Your manager has identified a few errors in the original data. Make the following amendments, and ensure that the **INCOME** figures are updated as a result of these changes. a The **SCOTLAND** figure for **GB1682** should be **48415** b The **COST** figure for **TY3090** should be **49.95** c **ITEM CODE TY3093** is incorrect, it should be **TY3092** d The **ENGLAND** figure for **WP307** should be **21090**
4a, 4b	10	Apply alignment as follows: a The row labels (**ITEM CODE** to **WP307**) should be left-aligned. b The column headings (**SCOTLAND** to **INCOME**) should be right-aligned. c All numeric data should be right-aligned.
4c, 4d, 4e	11	Format the data as follows: a All the figures from **SCOTLAND** to **TOTAL** should be displayed in integer format (0 decimal places). b The **COST** and **VAT** figures should be displayed to 2 decimal places. c The **INCOME** figures should be displayed with a £ sign and to 2 decimal places.
5c, 5e	12	Save your spreadsheet using a new filename and print one copy showing the values (figures) not the formulae. Ensure that all the data is displayed in full.
5d	13	Print the spreadsheet with all formulae showing. Ensure that all the formulae are displayed in full.
1a, 5f	14	Close your spreadsheet and exit the software securely.

Self-assessment: Task 4

Did I do it correctly?

☐ Loaded your spreadsheet application and created a new spreadsheet

☐ Entered the text and numerical data (leaving the **VAT** and **INCOME** columns blank) and put your name, centre number and the date below the data

☐ Inserted the new column **TOTAL** between the columns **WALES** and **COST**

☐ Insert formulae to calculate the **TOTAL, VAT** and **INCOME** for item code **GB1681** and replicated them for each of the other item codes

☐ Changed:
  - the **SCOTLAND** figure for **GB1682** to **48415**
  - the **COST** figure for **TY3090** to **49.95**
  - corrected the item code to **TY3092**
  - the **ENGLAND** figure for **WP307** to **21090**

☐ Deleted the column containing the data for **IRELAND**

☐ Checked that the **INCOME** figures were updated as a result of the changes to the data

☐ Applied alignment as follows:
  - **left** to the row labels from **ITEM CODE** to **WP307**
  - **right** to the column headings from **SCOTLAND** to **INCOME**
  - **right** to all numeric data

☐ Applied the following formatting:
  - **integer** to all the figures from **SCOTLAND** to **TOTAL**
  - **2 decimal places** to the **COST** and **VAT** figures
  - **currency** (£ sign and 2 decimal places) to the **INCOME** figures

☐ Saved your spreadsheet

☐ Saved your spreadsheet using a new filename

☐ Printed a copy of your spreadsheet showing the values (figures) in full

☐ Printed a copy of your spreadsheet with all formulae showing in full

☐ Closed your spreadsheet and exited the software securely

TASK 5

This task allows you to practise a complete OCR Level 1 Certificate for IT Users (NEW CLAIT) assignment. It covers all the OCR Level 1 Certificate for IT Users (NEW CLAIT) spreadsheets assessment objectives.

Scenario

You work as an administrative assistant for Progress Excursions. You are responsible for a variety of tasks, including production of routine financial reports.

What You Have To Do

Assessment Objectives		
		Your manager has asked you to produce a spreadsheet report showing the number of excursions sold at the company's sites.
Ia, 5a	I	Load your spreadsheet application and create a new spreadsheet.
2a	2	Enter the following data, leaving the **TOTAL INCOME** column blank.

BRANCH	MON	TUE	WED	THU	FRI	PRICE	BRANCH FEE	TOTAL INCOME
BLACKMOOR	1295	1574	1498	1599	1022	1.5	6.5	
BRIDGEMERE	3465	3409	3844	3901	4200	2.65	3.5	
IMPERIAL	780	584	358	157	720	5.99	9.35	
SOUTHWICK	5643	5840	5820	5022	5493	5.99	3.85	
COURTLAND	3548	3744	3090	3755	3975	5.75	7.5	
RABY	2077	2535	2755	2855	2954	5	8.53	
THURSTASTON	4766	4933	5011	4989	4935	6.55	4.65	
THIRLMERE	3766	3099	3964	3854	3909	4.99	5	

2a, 5b	3	Enter your name, centre number and today's date below the data and print one copy showing the figures. Ensure that all the data is shown in full.
2a, 2b	4	Insert a new column entitled **WEEK TOTAL** between the columns **FRI** and **PRICE**.
3a, 3b	5	**WEEK TOTAL** is the sum of the figures from **MON** to **FRI**. Insert a formula to calculate the **WEEK TOTAL** for **BLACKMOOR**. Replicate this formula to show the **WEEK TOTAL** for each of the other branches.
3a, 3b	6	**TOTAL INCOME** is calculated by multiplying the **WEEK TOTAL** by **PRICE** and then adding the **BRANCH FEE**. Insert a formula to calculate the **TOTAL INCOME** for **BLACKMOOR**. Replicate this formula to show the **TOTAL INCOME** for each of the other branches.
2c	7	The **IMPERIAL** figures are actually part of the total for Bridgemere, and should not be shown separately. Delete the entire row for **IMPERIAL**.
2d, 3c	8	Your manager has identified a few errors in the original data. Make the following amendments, and ensure that the **TOTAL INCOME** figures are updated as a result of these changes.
		a The **WED** figure for **SOUTHWICK** should be **5802**
		b The **BRANCH FEE** for **RABY** should be **8.35**
		c The **FRI** figure for **THURSTASTON** should be **4035**
		d **THIRLMOOR** has been entered incorrectly as **THIRLMERE**.

What You Have To Do

Assessment Objectives		
4a, 4b	9	Apply alignment as follows: **a** The row labels (**BRANCH** to **THIRLMOOR**) should be left-aligned. **b** The column headings (**MON** to **TOTAL INCOME**) should be right-aligned. **c** All numeric data should be right-aligned.
4c, 4d, 4e	10	Format the data as follows: **a** All the figures from **MON** to **WEEK TOTAL** should be displayed in integer format (0 decimal places). **b** The **PRICE** and **BRANCH FEE** figures should be displayed to 2 decimal places. **c** The **TOTAL INCOME** figures should be displayed with a £ sign and to 2 decimal places.
5c, 5e	11	Save your spreadsheet using a new filename and print one copy showing the values (figures) not the formulae. Ensure that all the data is displayed in full.
5d	12	Print the spreadsheet with all formulae showing. Ensure that all the formulae are displayed in full.
1a, 5f	13	Close your spreadsheet and exit the software securely.

Self-assessment: Task 5

Did I do it correctly?

- ☐ Loaded the spreadsheet application
- ☐ Entered the text and numerical data
- ☐ Inserted a new column
- ☐ Deleted the specified row
- ☐ Amended the specified text and numerical data
- ☐ Entered and replicated formulae
- ☐ Recalculated data
- ☐ Displayed text left-aligned
- ☐ Displayed text right-aligned
- ☐ Displayed numerical data right-aligned
- ☐ Displayed numeric data in integer format (to 0 decimal places)
- ☐ Displayed numeric data to 2 decimal places
- ☐ Displayed numerical data in currency format (to include £ sign)
- ☐ Saved the spreadsheet
- ☐ Saved the spreadsheet with a new filename
- ☐ Printed the spreadsheet display
- ☐ Printed the formulae used in the spreadsheet
- ☐ Closed the spreadsheet.

UNIT 5 Databases Overview

What is a database?

A database is **an organised collection of information** which makes use of a computer's ability to store data. It could be described as an 'electronic filing system'. Databases can range from small collections of information, such as the names, addresses and telephone numbers of customers, to large collections of data, such as the owners, car registration numbers, and type of registered car vehicles in the UK.

Why use a database system?

The information stored in a database is structured so that you can search and sort the information quickly and accurately. A database program will provide you with a fast means of finding and retrieving the information you need.

Organisation

You need to be familiar with the following terms:

File

Each set of related records is called a file.

Record

Each collection of data for each item in the file is known as a record. The data needs to be set up in the same format for each item in the collection.

Field

The data in each record is stored under headings known as fields.

It may help to consider an example of these terms. An estate agency will need to keep a database of the houses it has for sale. The data stored is likely to include the name and address of the person selling the property, the area, price, number of rooms, type of heating.

The file will be the complete collection, ie for all the properties being dealt with by the estate agency, a record will be the set of details about one property in the collection, and a field will be one of the headings, eg name of seller or price.

Once the data has been entered, any details which change can be updated, if there are more houses to be sold they can be added as new records, and if any houses are sold then those records can be deleted.

Types of field

In order for the computer to retrieve the information as quickly and efficiently as possible, you need to store the data in the best way for retrieval. To help you do this there are different types of field structures:

Alphabetic

Data stored in alphabetic fields will allow you to produce alphabetic lists of information. Alphabetic fields recognise letters of the alphabet.

Field

Record

File

Microsoft Access - [CLIENTS : Table]

File Edit View Insert Format Records Tools Window Help

CLIENT CODE	TITLE	SURNAME	FIRST NAME	COMPANY	ADDRESS 1	ADDRESS 2
AB-01	Ms	Butler	Annette		12 The Grove	
AB-02	Miss	Angela	Barlowe		The Cottage	12 Vicarage Street
BI-01	Mr	Mahesh	Patel	Big Insurance Co	Business House	12-16 Bath Road
CR-01	Mr	Rayner	Charles		Flat 12	High View
JS-01	Mr	Smith	John		Yew Tree Cottage	5 Bisley Road
ME-01	Ms	Desai	Manjit	Munroe Estate Agents	23 High Street	
SM-01	Mrs	Mainwaring	Sally		10 The Park	

Numeric

Data stored in numeric fields will allow you to produce lists in ascending or descending order. Some databases will also allow you to carry out arithmetical tasks. Numeric fields recognise numbers.

Alphanumeric

Data stored in alphanumeric fields will allow you to produce alphabetic lists. It is the normal field type (which includes numeric data that does not need to be sorted numerically, eg telephone numbers).

Alphanumeric fields recognise both letters and numbers.

Date

Date fields allow you to enter data in a number of formats. There is also a facility that allows for a 'time' element to be added in this type of field.

Finding data

Sorting

When you sort the data stored in a database the records will be put in order.

You can sort alphabetic fields in alphabetic order, eg a list of property sellers with family name/surname from A to Z, and the numeric data in a list of ascending or descending order, eg a list of prices from the lowest to highest, or highest to lowest price.

Searching

You can use a database to find a particular item of information. For example, you could look for a house in a particular area, eg Newtown, and the search will produce a list of all the houses in the file in Newtown. This is known as a search on one criterion – in this case **AREA**.

It is also possible to search on more than one criterion, eg you could search for all the houses in the file in the area of Newtown costing more than £45,000.

Displaying and printing information

The information stored in a database can be displayed on the screen as required. You can also print the information. Your package will determine how this is done but you will probably be able to choose whether to:

- print all the data in the file record by record
- print all the data in the file in columns under the field headings
- print specified data either for all the data, for selected records or data from selected fields for all or some of the records.

Helping you pass

Critical errors

- Incorrect search results
- Missing field(s)

Accuracy errors

- Check the data you have entered as **data errors contained in each field** will count as a separate accuracy error.
- Check that you have completed all the objectives as each one not met will count as a separate error.

Tips

- Check that all the fields are wide enough to display all the data.
- Make sure that you have sorted the correct field and that it is in the correct order (ascending or descending).

Build Up Exercises

TASK 1

This task is designed to allow you to practise the skills required to gain OCR Level 1 Certificate for IT Users (NEW CLAIT) assessment objectives.

Before you begin

You will need to find out and note down how to:

- switch on your system
- load your database application
- open an existing database
- enter new records
- enter data
- replace specified data
- save data
- print data in table format.

There is a checklist for you to complete on page 65 to use as a reference sheet.

You will also need the data file **appliances**.

You will find the **appliances** file on the CD supplied with this book.

Scenario

You work as an administrator for Progress Appliances. The company has three outlets, one in England, one in Scotland and one in Wales. Your duties include maintenance of the database that holds customer purchase information. You can assume that a customer will purchase goods in the town in which they live.

What You Have To Do

Assessment Objectives		
1a, 5a	1	You have been asked to amend the database and provide some routine reports. Start your database application and open the database **appliances**.
2a, 2b, 2c	2	Two of the sales receipts had been omitted and one of the sales was cancelled. Create records for the two sales as follows:

a   **ERIC JONES** who lives at **6 FIELD WAY, KIRKLAND** bought a **DISHWASHER (CODE 55470)** on **5 January 2001**. It cost **£299.50**.

b   **ELAINE JAMES** who lives at **56 WELDON WAY, WELDON** bought a **MICROWAVE (CODE 20900)** on **6 January 2001**. It cost **£435.99**.

c   Delete the record for the sale of the **DISHWASHER** to **AMANDA WINTER** in **WELDON**.

What You Have To Do

Assessment Objectives		
2e	3	Some of the repetitive data would be more efficiently stored encoded.
		In the **PRODUCT** field, replace the existing data as follows:
		a **TUMBLE DRYER** should be replaced with **TD**
		b **DISHWASHER** should be replaced with **DW**
		c **MICROWAVE** should be replaced with **MW**
		d **WASHING MACHINE** should be replaced with **WM**
5b, 5d	4	Save your file and print all the data in table format. Ensure that all the data is displayed in full.

TASK 2

This task is designed to allow you to practise the skills required to gain OCR Level 1 Certificate for IT Users (NEW CLAIT) assessment objectives.

Before you begin

You will need to find out and note down how to:

- select data on one criterion
- present only selected fields
- sort data alphabetically
- save query/filter
- print your data in table format.

What You Have To Do

Assessment Objectives		
	1	Reload the database file saved in Task 1.
3a, 3c, 4a	2	At the time of the sales the store in Kirkland had run out of the contracts for extended warranty cover on appliances. These contracts have to be sent to the customers.
		Set up the following query:
		a Select all appliances sold in **KIRKLAND**.
		b Sort the data in ascending alphabetical order of **PRODUCT**.
		c Display *only* the **NAME**, **ADDRESS**, **PRODUCT** and **COST £** fields.
5c, 5d	3	Save your query and print the results in table format.

TASK 3

This task is designed to allow you to practise the skills required to gain OCR Level 1 Certificate for IT Users (NEW CLAIT) assessment objectives.

Before you begin

You will need to find out and note down how to:

- amend data
- select data on two criteria
- sort data numerically and by date
- save data
- close database.

What You Have To Do

Assessment Objectives		
	I	Reload the database file saved in Task 1.
2d	2	Some errors have been found in the data entered. Please make these amendments. **a** DENNIS MORTON lives at **90** not **9** BLACKEND ROAD. **b** The WASHING MACHINE bought by DENNIS BEST cost **£299.50**.
3b, 4c	3	A fault has been reported with a batch of dishwashers. They were sold only at the Kirkland branch. Set up the following query: **a** Search for any **DISHWASHER** bought in **KIRKLAND**. **b** Sort the data in ascending order of **PURCHASE DATE** (ie earliest date first). **c** Display *only* the **NAME, ADDRESS, COST £** and **PURCHASE DATE** fields.
5c, 5d	4	Save your query and print the results in table format, ensuring that the data is fully displayed.
3b, 4b	5	It has been noted that some of the prices of appliances sold at the Shepton branch were incorrect. Set up the following query: **a** Search for any appliance bought in **SHEPTON**. **b** Sort the data in ascending numerical order of **PRODUCT CODE** (ie lowest number first). **c** Display *only* the **PRODUCT CODE, PRODUCT** and **COST £** fields.
5b, 5c, 5d 5e	6	Save your query and print the results in table format, ensuring that the data is fully displayed. Save your file and close the database application in the correct sequence with the data secure.

Databases Checklist

You should complete this checklist for each hardware and software combination you use. Use information from your tutor, handouts, handbooks and software manuals to complete the list. You can then use your list as a reference sheet to complete the practice tasks that follow.

Hardware: _____

Software: _____

ASSESSMENT OBJECTIVE	HOW TO DO IT	OCR REFERENCE
1 Identify and use database software correctly		
Use appropriate application software	_____	1a
2 Use an input device to enter and edit data accurately		
Create new records	_____	2a
Enter data	_____	2b
Delete record	_____	2c
Amend data	_____	2d
Replace specified data	_____	2e
3 Create simple queries/searches on one or two criteria		
Select data on one criterion	_____	3a
Select data on two criteria	_____	3b
Present only selected fields	_____	3c
4 Present selected data sorted alphabetically, numerically and by date		
Sort data alphabetically	_____	4a
Sort data numerically	_____	4b
Sort data by date	_____	4c
5 Manage and print database files		
Open an existing database	_____	5a
Save data	_____	5b
Save query/filter	_____	5c
Print data in table format	_____	5d
Close database	_____	5e

OCR Assignments and Self-Assessments

This task allows you to practise a complete OCR Level 1 Certificate for IT Users (NEW CLAIT) assignment. It covers all the OCR Level 1 Certificate for IT Users (NEW CLAIT) databases assessment objectives.

Scenario

You work as an administrator for Progress Engineering plc. Your duties include maintenance of the staff database.

You will need the data file **staff**.

You will find the **staff** file on the CD supplied with this book.

What You Have To Do

Assessment Objectives		
		You have been asked to amend the database and provide specified reports.
1a, 5a	1	Start your database application and open the database **staff**.
2a, 2b, 2c	2	Two new members of staff have joined the company, and one has left.

Create records for the new members of staff as follows:

a **JONES, L** joined the **ENGINEERING** department in **DONCASTER** as an **ADMINISTRATOR** on **2 October, 2001**. Her staff number is **ED417**, and her security grade **10**.

b **WATSON, H** joined the **SALES** department in **ALLPORT** as an **ADMINISTRATOR** on **4 October, 2001**. His staff number is **SA910**, and his security grade **10**.

c Delete the record for **ROBINSON, E** from the **ENGINEERING** department in **DONCASTER** as he has left the company.

What You Have To Do

Assessment Objectives		
2e	3	Some of the repetitive data would be more efficiently stored encoded. In the **DEPARTMENT** field, replace the existing data as follows: a **ACCOUNTS** should be replaced with **A** b **ENGINEERING** should be replaced with **E** c **IT** should be replaced with **I** d **SALES** should be replaced with **S**
5b, 5d	4	Save your file and print all the data in table format. Ensure that all the data is displayed in full.
3a, 3c 4a	5	It has been decided that the security grading should be re-assessed. Set up the following query: a Select all staff who have a **SECURITY GRADE** below **20**. b Sort the data in ascending alphabetical order of **STAFF NO**. c Display *only* the following fields: **DEPARTMENT, STAFF NO, JOB TITLE** and **SECURITY GRADE**.
5c, 5d	6	Save your query and print the results in table format.
2d	7	There have been some changes following the security review. Make the following amendments to the **SECURITY GRADE** data for: a **BAINS, O** from 10 to **15**. b **HOBSON**, S from 15 to **18**.
3b, 3c, 4b	8	The engineering group in Allport have exceeded their sales targets and have been awarded a special bonus. Set up the following query: a Select all staff who work in the **ENGINEERING (E)** department in **ALLPORT**. b Sort the data in ascending numerical order of **SECURITY GRADE** (ie lowest number first). c Display *only* the **NAME, JOB TITLE, SECURITY GRADE** and **START DATE** fields.
5c, 5d	9	Save your query and print the results in table format, ensuring that the data is fully displayed.
3a, 3c, 4a	10	Following a problem with the computer system at the Allport site, there is doubt regarding the validity of the data held. Set up the following query: a Select all staff who work at **ALLPORT**. b Sort the data in ascending order of **START DATE** (ie earliest date first). c Display *only* the **STAFF NUMBER, NAME** and **START DATE** fields.
5c, 5d	11	Save your query and print the results in table format, ensuring that the data is fully displayed.
1a, 5b, 5e	12	Save your file and close the database application in the correct sequence with the data secure.

Self-assessment: Task 4

Did I do it correctly?

☐ Loaded the database application

☐ Opened the specified database file

☐ Added the records

☐ Deleted the record

☐ Replaced specified data

☐ Searched for records for security grades below **20**

☐ Searched for staff in the **Allport** engineering department

☐ Searched for staff in **Allport**

☐ Sorted the records into ascending numerical order of **security grade**

☐ Sorted the records into ascending alphabetical order or **staff number**

☐ Sorted the records into ascending order of start date

☐ Saved the data and the queries

☐ Printed the data in table format, ie in columns across the page

☐ Printed selected fields in table format

☐ Ensured that data was secure and exited from the database application.

TASK 5

This task allows you to practise a complete OCR Level 1 Certificate for IT Users (NEW CLAIT) assignment. It covers all the OCR Level 1 Certificate for IT Users (NEW CLAIT) databases assessment objectives.

Scenario

You work as an administrator for Progress Motor Company. Your duties include maintenance of the used cars database.

You will need the data file **cars**.

You will find the **cars** file on the CD supplied with this book.

What You Have To Do

Assessment Objectives		You have been asked to amend the database and provide some routine reports.
1a, 5a	1	Start your database application and open the database **cars**.
2a, 2b, 2c	2	Four new cars have been bought and one has been sold.

Create records for the new cars as follows:

a   5 door **FORD ESCORT** registered in **March 2000**. It is **SILVER** and has mileage of **21000**. The cost is **£6495**.

b   5 door **FORD FIESTA** registered in **February 1998**. It is **WHITE** and has mileage of **54000**. The cost is **£6995**.

c   5 door **FORD GRANADA** registered in **June 1995**. It is **WHITE** and has mileage of **73000**. The cost is **£3995**.

d   5 door **FORD GRANADA** registered in **February 1996**. It is **RED** and has mileage of **64000**. The cost is **£4955**.

e   Delete the record for the **VAUXHALL TIGRA**.

What You Have To Do

Assessment Objectives		
2e	3	Some of the repetitive data would be more efficiently stored encoded. In the **MAKE** field, replace the existing data as follows: a **FORD** should be replaced with **F** b **PEUGEOT** should be replaced with **P** c **VAUXHALL** should be replaced with **V**
5b, 5d	4	Save your file and print all the data in table format. Ensure that all the data is displayed in full.
3a, 3c, 4b	5	A customer has enquired about a car, the main requirement being 3 door. Set up the following query: a Select all cars that are **3** door. b Sort the data in ascending numerical order of **COST (£)**, ie lowest price first. c Display *only* the following fields: **MAKE, MODEL, MILEAGE, COLOUR, REGISTERED** and **COST(£)**.
5c, 5d	6	Save your query and print the results in table format.
2d	7	Some of the car details are incorrect. Make the following amendments: a The **GREEN FORD MONDEO** registered in **July 1999** should display a cost of **£7995** not £7795. b The **GREEN FORD FOCUS** registered in **November 1999** should display mileage of **20000** not 19000.
3b, 3c 4a	8	A customer has enquired about Ford cars that do not have high mileage. Set up the following query: a Select all **FORD (F)** cars with mileage below **25000**. b Sort the data in ascending order of **MODEL**. c Display only the following fields: **MODEL, MILEAGE, DOORS, REGISTERED** and **COST (£)**.
5c, 5d	9	Save your query and print the results in table format, ensuring that the data is fully displayed.
3a, 3c, 4c	10	A customer has enquired about Vauxhall cars. Set up the following query: a Select all **VAUXHALL** cars. b Sort the data in ascending order of the **REGISTERED** date (ie earliest date first). c Display *only* the following fields: **MODEL , MILEAGE, COLOUR, DOORS, REGISTERED** and **COST(£)**.
5c, 5d	11	Save your query and print the results in table format, ensuring that the data is fully displayed.
1a, 5b, 5e	12	Save your file and close the database application in the correct sequence with the data secure.

Self-assessment: Task 5

Did I do it correctly?

☐ Loaded the database application

☐ Opened the specified database file

☐ Added the records

☐ Deleted the record

☐ Replaced specified data

☐ Searched for records

☐ Sorted the records keeping numerical order

☐ Sorted the records into alphabetical order and by date

☐ Saved the data

☐ Saved the queries

☐ Printed the data in table format, ie in columns across the page

☐ Printed selected fields in table format

☐ Ensured that data is secure and exited from the database application.

UNIT 6 Desktop Publishing Overview

What is desktop publishing (DTP)?

A DTP package combines text, graphics, design elements and printing facilities. It is a fast and effective means of producing and printing material in a variety of layouts and styles.

Why use a DTP package?

The package allows you to display information in a variety of formats similar to those of professional typesetters and designers. You can use a DTP package to produce notices, newsletters, advertisements, magazine articles, books or any other material that needs to be displayed effectively.

Stages in producing a document using a DTP package

This is the usual way of producing a document using a DTP package, but of course variations are possible. The manner in which you produce your document will depend on the features of your package and your own way of working.

STEP 1 Produce the text

This is usually prepared using a word processing package to create a file which can then be inserted into the DTP package. There is sometimes a word processing facility within the DTP package.

STEP 2 Prepare the graphics (images)

Graphics or illustrations can be produced using a graphics/drawing package or within the graphics facility of the DTP package.

There are alternative methods of producing graphics – you can use a scanner to convert photographs or drawings into a computer data file or you can use pre-prepared images from a clip art facility.

STEP 3 Design the layout and style

You load the pre-prepared text and graphics and edit or amend the layout until you are satisfied with the result.

Remember: at any stage of the process the contents and layout of the document can be edited, amended or altered. The document can be saved and recalled at a later date.

Basic display features of a DTP package

The basic display features of your DTP package will normally include the ability to control the:

- page size
- position of the text and images
- number and width of columns
- use of borders and/or boxes
- use of font types and sizes
- text display features such as centring and alignment.

Desktop publishing terms

Clip art

A collection or 'library' of pre-prepared graphics that can be used within a document. Commonly used pictures are sometimes included with your DTP package. Others can be bought as required and are available on a variety of topics.

Fonts

The 'style' and shape of printed characters. Fonts have names by which they can be recognised, eg **Times New Roman**, **Arial**, **Book Antigua**. The choice of font can be very important because of the message it can convey to the reader.

Alignment

The text can be left-aligned, right-aligned, centred or justified. When text is justified it is arranged so that it is presented straight at both the left-hand and right-hand margins.

Mouse

A device for controlling the position of the cursor on the screen. It provides a quick and easy means of identifying and moving images or text when editing or amending. You control the cursor by a combination of clicking the buttons on the mouse to identify the area and 'dragging' the image or text to the new position required.

Point size

A unit for measuring print size. There are 72 points to an inch. You usually use different point sizes to display the heading, sub-headings, and the main body of the text.

Sans-serif font

A font which does not have short strokes from the main lines of the character. These are modern fonts.

Serif font

A font which does have short strokes from the main lines of the character. These are traditional fonts.

Template

A prepared layout which can be set up by the package or which you can set up for yourself. It can be stored for use over and over again and will provide consistency of layout for documents.

Helping you pass

Critical errors

- A missing image.
- An incorrect text file imported.

Accuracy errors

- **The heading only** will count as one separate accuracy error. The imported text is not assessed for accuracy.
- Check that you have completed all the objectives as each one not met will count as a separate error.

Tips

- Check that you have balanced the columns – the longest column can be no more than two lines short of the bottom margin and the other column can be no more than two lines short of the first column.
- To help balance the column, adjust the space below the heading, above and/or below the subheadings and/or images.

Build Up Exercises

This task is designed to allow you to practise the skills required to gain OCR Level 1 Certificate for IT Users (NEW CLAIT) assessment objectives.

Before you begin

You will need to find out and note down how to:

- load your desktop publishing application
- create a new publication
- set page size/orientation
- set margins
- save master page/template.

There is a checklist for you to complete on page 77 to use as a reference sheet.

You will also need the data file **passport** and the image file **travel**.

You will find the **passport** and **travel** files on the CD supplied with this book.

		What You Have To Do
Assessment Objectives		**You have been asked to produce an A4 information leaflet for travellers.**
Ia, 5a	I	Load your DTP application, and create a new single-page publication.
2a, 2b	2	Set up the master page or template for the page as follows:
		page size: **A4**
		page orientation: **portrait (tall)**
		top/bottom margins: **2.5 cm**
		left/right margins: **2 cm**
5b	3	Save master page/template.

TASK 2

This task is designed to allow you to practise the skills required to gain OCR Level 1 Certificate for IT Users (NEW CLAIT) assessment objectives.

Before you begin

You will need to find out and note down how to:

- create text areas/text frames
- set column widths/spacing
- use serif and sans-serif fonts
- import text file(s)
- import image(s)
- enter a heading
- fit the headline text to page width
- apply alignment and justification
- save publication
- print composite proofs.

What You Have To Do

Assessment Objectives		
2c, 2d	1	Using the master page or template saved in Task 1, set up the page layout in a leaflet format, to include a page-wide heading above two columns of text. column widths: **equal** space between columns: **1.5 cm**
2e, 3c	2	Key in the heading **TRAVELLING ABROAD?** at the top of the page, using a **sans-serif** font.
4e	3	Increase the size of the heading text so that it extends across the full width of both columns of text.
3b	4	Import the image **travel**, and place it at the top of the left-hand column, below the heading.
3a	5	Import the text file **passport** so that it begins below the image in the left-hand column.
2e, 4a	6	Format the body text to be left-aligned, in a **serif** font.
5c, 5d	7	Save the publication, and print one composite proof copy. Make sure that your publication fits onto one page.

TASK 3

This task is designed to allow you to practise the skills required to gain OCR Level 1 Certificate for IT Users (NEW CLAIT) assessment objectives.

Before you begin

You will need to find out and note down how to:

- use 3 font sizes (large, medium and small)
- use line or border features
- set paragraph spacing and/or first line indent
- move a graphics image to a new position
- resize text
- balance the text/images in columns
- close your publication.

What You Have To Do

Assessment Objectives		You are to make the following amendments to the publication.
	I	Reload the file saved in Task 2.
3d	2	Draw a line below the heading separating it from the graphic and the columns of text. The line should extend from the left-hand margin to the right-hand margin.
4d	3	Increase the size of the subheadings **Safety** and **Visas** so that they are larger than the body text, but smaller than the page heading.
4c	4	Change the position of the graphic from the top of the left-hand column, to the bottom of the left-hand column. Make sure that the image does not extend into any margin space.
4a	5	Change the body text to be **fully justified**.
4b	6	Format the body text so that the first line of each paragraph is indented. Make sure that the subheadings are *not* included.
2f, 4d, 4f	7	Increase the size of the body text so that the columns are balanced at the bottom of the page.
		Ensure that:
		• the text starts from the top of the first column, replacing the image
		• the image is placed at the bottom of the left-hand column
		• the body text, subheadings and heading are still each displayed in a clearly different type size (ie small, medium and large)
		• no text is lost from the page.
5c, 5d	8	Save the publication and print a composite proof. Make sure your publication fits onto one page.
5e	9	Close your publication and exit the software securely.

Desktop Publishing Checklist

You should complete this checklist for each hardware and software combination you use. Use information from your tutor, handouts, handbooks and software manuals to complete the list. You can then use your list as a reference sheet to complete the practice tasks that follow.

Hardware: _____

Software: _____

ASSESSMENT OBJECTIVE	HOW TO DO IT	OCR REFERENCE
1 Identify and use appropriate software correctly		
Use appropriate application software		1a
2 Set up a standard page layout and text properties		
Set page size/orientation		2a
Set margins		2b
Create text areas/text frames		2c
Set column widths/spacing		2d
Use serif/sans-serif fonts		2e
Use multiple font sizes		2f
3 Import and place text and image files		
Import text file(s)		3a
Import image(s)		3b
Enter heading		3c
Use line or border feature		3d
4 Manipulate text and images to balance page		
Apply alignment and justification		4a
Set paragraph spacing and/or first line indent		4b
Move/resize image		4c
Resize text		4d
Fit headline text to page width		4e
Balance columns		4f
5 Manage publications and print composite proofs		
Create new publication		5a
Save master page/template		5b
Save publication		5c
Print composite proof(s)		5d
Close publication		5e

OCR Assignments and Self-Assessments

TASK 4

This task allows you to practise a complete OCR Level 1 Certificate for IT Users (NEW CLAIT) assignment. It covers all the OCR Level 1 Certificate for IT Users (NEW CLAIT) desktop publishing assessment objectives.

You will also need the data file **history** and the image file **historypic**.

You will find the **history** and **historypic** files on the CD supplied with this book.

What You Have To Do

Assessment Objectives		You have been asked to produce an A4 information leaflet about desktop publishing.
1a, 5a	1	Load your DTP application, and create a new single-page publication.
2a, 2b	2	Set up the master page or template for the page as follows: page size: **A4** page orientation: **portrait (tall)** top/bottom margins: **2.5 cm** left/right margins: **2 cm**
5b	3	Save master page/template.
2c, 2d	4	Set up the page layout in a leaflet format, to include a page-wide heading above two columns of text. column widths: **equal** space between columns: **1.5 cm**
2e, 3c	5	Key in the heading **DESKTOP PUBLISHING** at the top of the page, using a **serif** font.
4e	6	Increase the size of the heading text so that it extends across the full width of both columns of text.
3a	7	Import the text file **history** so that it begins at the top of the left-hand column, below the heading.
2e, 4a	8	Format the body text to be left-aligned, in a **sans-serif** font.
3b	9	Import the image **historypic**, and place it at the bottom of the right-hand column, below the text.
5c, 5d	10	Save the publication, and print one composite proof copy. Make sure that all the text is displayed and that your publication fits onto one page.
		You are to make the following amendments to the publication.
3d	11	Draw a box around the heading.

What You Have To Do

Assessment Objectives		
4d	12	Increase the size of the subheadings **History** and **Today** so that they are larger than the body text, but smaller than the page heading. Ensure that the subheadings are left-aligned and displayed in a **serif** font.
4c	13	Move the image from the bottom of the right-hand column, to the bottom of the left-hand column. Make sure that the image does not extend into any margin space.
4a	14	Change the body text to be **fully justified**.
4b	15	Format the body text so that the first line of each paragraph is indented. Make sure that the subheadings are *not* included
2f, 4d, 4f	16	Increase the size of the body text so that the columns are balanced at the bottom of the page.

Ensure that:
- the text starts from the top of the first column
- the image is placed at the bottom of the left-hand column
- the body text, subheadings and heading are still each displayed in a clearly different type size (ie small, medium and large)
- no text is lost from the page.

5c, 5d	17	Save the publication and print a composite proof. Make sure your publication fits onto one page.
1a, 5e	18	Close your publication and exit the software securely.

Self-assessment: Task 4

Did I do it correctly?

- [ ] Started up the system and loaded the DTP application
- [ ] Created an A4 page layout with a page-wide heading and two-column display
- [ ] Entered the heading **DESKTOP PUBLISHING** in a large type size and serif font
- [ ] Put the headline text to fit page width
- [ ] Drew a box around the heading
- [ ] Imported the prepared text file
- [ ] Set the body text for the imported file in a small type size and left alignment
- [ ] Imported the prepared graphic image and placed it at the bottom of the right-hand column
- [ ] Saved and printed the document
- [ ] Changed the size of the subheadings **History** and **Today**
- [ ] Altered the body text so that it is fully justified
- [ ] Moved the graphic image
- [ ] Changed the size of the body text to fill the A4 page, ensuring no loss of text
- [ ] Saved and printed the final document
- [ ] Closed the publication.

TASK 5

This task allows you to practise a complete OCR Level 1 Certificate for IT Users (NEW CLAIT) assignment. It covers all the OCR Level 1 Certificate for IT Users (NEW CLAIT) desktop publishing assessment objectives.

You will also need the data file **buenavista** and the image file **buenapic**.

You will find the **buenavista** and **buenapic** files on the CD supplied with this book.

What You Have To Do

Assessment Objectives		
		You have been asked to produce an A4 advertising release about a new holiday site for members of a holiday club.
1a, 5a	1	Load your DTP application, and create a new single-page publication.
2a, 2b	2	Set up the master page or template for the page as follows: page size: **A4** page orientation: **portrait (tall)** top/bottom margins: **2.5 cm** left/right margins: **2.5 cm**
5b	3	Save master page/template.
2c, 2d	4	Set up the page layout in a leaflet format, to include a page-wide heading above two columns of text. column widths: **equal** space between columns: **1 cm**
2e, 3c	5	Key in the heading **BUENA VISTA** at the top of the page, using a **serif** font.
4e	6	Increase the size of the heading text so that it extends across the full width of both columns of text.
3b	7	Import the image **buenapic**, and place it at the top of the left-hand column, below the heading.
3a	8	Import the text file **buenavista** so that it begins below the image in the left-hand column.
2e, 4a	9	Format the body text to be left-aligned, in a **sans-serif** font.
5c, 5d	10	Save the publication, and print one composite proof copy. Make sure that all the text is displayed and that your publication fits onto one page.
		You are to make the following amendments to the publication.
3d	11	Draw a line below the heading separating it from the columns of text and the image. The line should extend from the left-hand margin to the right-hand margin.

What You Have To Do

Assessment Objectives		
4d	12	Increase the size of the subheadings **Attractions** and **Facilities** so that they are larger than the body text, but smaller than the page heading. Ensure that the subheadings are left-aligned and displayed in a **serif** font.
4c	13	Move the image from the top of the left-hand column to the bottom of the left-hand column. Make sure that the image does not extend into any margin space.
4a	14	Change the body text to be **fully justified**.
4b	15	Format the body text so that the first line of each paragraph is indented. Make sure that the subheadings are *not* included.
2f, 4d, 4f	16	Increase the size of the body text so that the columns are balanced at the bottom of the page. Ensure that: • the text starts from the top of the first column • the image is placed at the bottom of the left-hand column • the body text, subheadings and heading are still each displayed in a clearly different type size (ie small, medium and large) • no text is lost from the page.
5c, 5d	17	Save the publication and print a composite proof. Make sure your publication fits onto one page.
1a, 5e	18	Close your publication and exit the software securely.

Self-assessment: Task 5

Did I do it correctly?

☐ Started up the system and loaded the DTP application

☐ Created an A4 page layout with a page-wide heading and two-column display

☐ Imported the prepared text file

☐ Imported the prepared graphic image

☐ Entered text with no errors

☐ Put the headline text to fit page width

☐ Justified text

☐ Used three type sizes

☐ Used serif and sans-serif fonts

☐ Drew box and/or lines

☐ Changed the size of text

☐ Changed the alignment

☐ Moved the graphic

☐ Changed the size of the body text to fill the A4 page, ensuring no loss of text

☐ Saved the publication

☐ Printed the publication

☐ Closed the publication.

UNIT 7 Graphs and Charts Overview

What is a graphical representation of data application?

It is a package that allows you to display and print numerical information in a pictorial form. The data can be input in a variety of ways via a spreadsheet or database or directly in a package especially designed for graphic display. The package will normally offer a variety of types of graph, chart or diagram. You can add text – as headings and labels – to your selected display.

Why use a graphical representation of data application?

A graphical representation of data application allows you to select data and display the information in a variety of formats. You can decide which method is best suited to display your data. Graphs and charts can be drawn and any changes or corrections made easily. You can adjust the size and scale of the display, and select patterns or colours for parts of your graph without the need to redraw it. Text can be added in a variety of fonts and sizes. Charts and graphs can be stored on disk, recalled and printed.

DECEMBER CAKE SALES	
Wedding	5
Birthday	15
Anniversary	3
Festival	44
Miscellaneous	18

Data

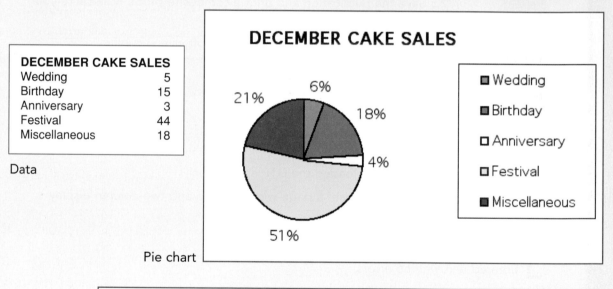

Pie chart

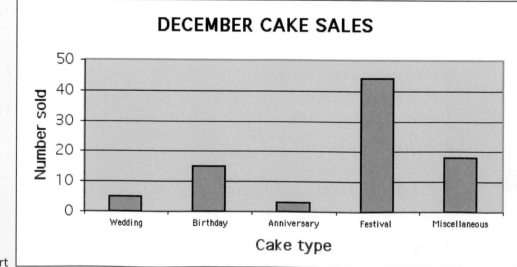

Bar chart

If displaying data this is how it would look on a pie chart and bar chart

TASK 2

This task is designed to allow you to practise the skills required to gain OCR Level 1 Certificate for IT Users (NEW CLAIT) assessment objectives.

Before you begin

You will need to find out and note down how to:

- use a bar/column chart
- select a subset of a single data set
- set upper axes limits
- set lower axes limits.

What You Have To Do

Assessment Objectives		
2c, 3c, 4a 4b, 4c	I	Your manager is hoping to make some savings. One of the areas where this may be possible is in the transport costs. Provide a bar chart showing this data for the last four months only (ie from March to June inclusive). Produce a bar chart showing the **TRANSPORT** figures from **MAR** to **JUN**. a Display the **months** along the x axis b Set the y-axis to display the range: **0** to **900** c Give the bar chart the heading: **TRANSPORT COSTS** d Label the x axis: **MONTH** e Label the y axis: **COSTS (£)**
5c	2	Save the bar chart.
5d	3	Print one copy of the bar chart.

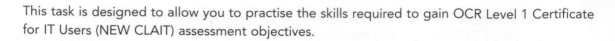

TASK 3

This task is designed to allow you to practise the skills required to gain OCR Level 1 Certificate for IT Users (NEW CLAIT) assessment objectives.

Before you begin

You will need to find out and note down how to:

- use a line graph
- select a comparative data set
- use a legend where appropriate
- save the data document.

		What You Have To Do
Assessment Objectives		
2b, 3b, 4a 4b, 4c, 4d 4e	1	Your manager is not sure that the savings can be made on transport alone, and would like you to produce a line graph comparing the costs for transport and utilities from January to June. Produce a line graph comparing the data for **TRANSPORT** and **UTILITIES** for **JAN** to **JUN**. **a** Display the **months** along the x axis **b** Set the y axis to display the range: **450** to **750** **c** Give the graph the heading: **TRANSPORT AND UTILITY COSTS** **d** Label the x axis: **MONTH** **e** Label the y axis: **COSTS (£)** **f** Use a legend to identify each line. Make sure that the lines and/or data points are distinctive, and can be identified when printed.
5c	2	Save the graph.
5d	3	Print one copy of the line graph.
5b	4	Save your data file.
1a, 5e	5	Close the document and exit the system securely.

Graphs and Charts Checklist

You should complete this checklist for each hardware and software combination you use. Use information from your tutor, handouts, handbooks and software manuals to complete the list. You can then use your list as a reference sheet to complete the practice tasks that follow.

Hardware: _____

Software: _____

ASSESSMENT OBJECTIVE	HOW TO DO IT	OCR REFERENCE
1 Identify and use appropriate software correctly		
Use appropriate application software	_____	Ia
2 Produce pie charts, line graphs and bar/column charts		
Use pie chart	_____	2a
Use line graph	_____	2b
Use bar/column chart	_____	2c
3 Select and present single and comparative sets of data		
Select a single data set	_____	3a
Select a comparative data set	_____	3b
Select a subset of a single data set	_____	3c
4 Set numerical parameters and format data		
Set axes' upper and lower limits	_____	4a
Select and display data labels	_____	4b
Select/enter headings and axes titles	_____	4c
Use a legend where appropriate	_____	4d
Ensure comparative data is distinctive	_____	4e
5 Manage and print graph and chart documents		
Open an existing data document	_____	5a
Save data document	_____	5b
Save charts/graphs	_____	5c
Print graphs/charts	_____	5d
Close document	_____	5e

OCR Assignments and Self-Assessments

TASK 4

This task allows you to practise a complete OCR Level 1 Certificate for IT Users (NEW CLAIT) assignment. It covers all the OCR Level 1 Certificate for IT Users (NEW CLAIT) graphs and charts assessment objectives.

Scenario

You work as an administrator for a health centre. Your duties include the production of weekly reports for your manager.

You will need the data file **DOCTORS** which is on the CD supplied with this book.

What You Have To Do

Assessment Objectives		
		Your manager has asked you to produce the set of reports in graph format showing patient and doctor activity during week 10.
la, 5a	I	Using application software that will allow you to produce graphs, open the data file **DOCTORS**, that contains details of the number of patients seen in week 10 by each of the doctors in the practice.
2a, 3a, 4b 4c, 4e	2	The first report will identify the number of patients seen by each of the doctors in week 10, using a pie chart.
		Create a pie chart to display the **TOTAL** for all of the doctors in week 10.
		a Give the chart the heading: **WEEK 10 PATIENT DISTRIBUTION**
		b Ensure that each segment is shaded in such a way that the data can be clearly identified (eg by pattern, colour or shade) when printed.
		c Each sector of the chart must be labelled clearly with the name of the doctor, and the **number** or **percentage** of patients.
5c	3	Save the pie chart.
5d	4	Print one copy of the pie chart.
2c, 3c, 4a	5	The second report will identify the number of patients seen by each of the doctors on Monday, in week 10. Do not include **DR HOEY**, who was on house calls that day.
		Produce a bar chart showing the **MON** figures for week 10 – excluding **HOEY**.
		a Display the **name of the doctor** along the x axis.
		b Set the y axis to display the range: **0 to 50**
		c Give the bar chart the heading: **NUMBER OF PATIENTS – MONDAY WEEK 10**
		d Label the x axis: **DOCTOR**
		e Label the y axis: **NO**

What You Have To Do

Assessment Objectives		
5c	6	Save the bar chart.
5d	7	Print one copy of the bar chart.
2b, 3b, 4a	8	The third report will identify the number of patients seen by **DR QUINN** and **DR WATSON** in week 10.
		Produce a line graph comparing the data for **QUINN** and **WATSON** for **MON** to **FRI**.
		a Display the **days** along the x axis.
		b Set the y axis to display the range: **0 to 60**
		c Give the graph the heading: **QUINN AND WATSON WEEK 10**
		d Label the x axis: **DAY**
		e Label the y axis: **NO OF PATIENTS**
		f Use a legend to identify each line. Make sure that the lines and/or data points are distinctive, and can be identified when printed.
5c	9	Save the graph.
5d	10	Print one copy of the line graph.
5b	11	Save your data file.
5e	12	Close the document and exit the software securely.

Self-assessment: Task 4

Did I do it correctly?

- [ ] Using suitable application software, opened the data file **DOCTORS**
- [ ] Using a single data set, created a pie chart to display the **TOTAL** for all the doctors in week 10
  - gave the chart the heading: **WEEK 10 PATIENT DISTRIBUTION**
  - clearly identified each segment
  - labelled each sector with a doctor's name, and the **number** or **percentage** of patients
- [ ] Using a subset of a single data set, produced a bar chart showing the number of patients seen by each of the doctors on Monday, in week 10, excluding DR HOEY
  - displayed the names of the doctors along the x axis
  - set the y axis to display the range: **0 to 50**
  - gave the bar chart the heading: **NO OF PATIENTS – MONDAY WEEK 10**
  - labelled the x axis: **DOCTOR and** the y axis: **NO**
- [ ] Using a comparative data set, produced a line graph showing the number of patients seen by doctors Quinn and Watson in week 10
  - displayed the **days** along the x axis
  - set the y axis to display the range: **0 to 60**
  - gave the graph the heading: **QUINN AND WATSON WEEK 10**
  - labelled the x axis: **DAY** and the y axis: **NO OF PATIENTS**
  - used a legend to identify each line, ensuring that they (or the data points) were distinctive
- [ ] Saved the data document; the pie chart; the bar chart; the line graph
- [ ] Printed the pie chart; the bar chart; the line graph
- [ ] Closed the data document and exited the software

TASK 5

This task allows you to practise a complete OCR Level 1 Certificate for IT Users (NEW CLAIT) assignment. It covers all the OCR Level 1 Certificate for IT Users (NEW CLAIT) graphs and charts assessment objectives.

Scenario

You work as an administrator for a council. Your duties include the production of graphical reports for your manager.

You will need the data file **RATES**.

You will find the **RATES** file on the CD supplied with this book.

Assessment Objectives		What You Have To Do
		Your manager has asked you to produce the set of reports in graph format showing council expenditure during the past five years.
1a, 5a	1	Using application software that will allow you to produce graphs, open the data file **RATES**, that contains details of expenditure on services for the last five years.
2a, 3a, 4b 4c, 4e	2	The first report will identify the spending on each of the services in 2001, using a pie chart.
		Create a pie chart to display the **2001** figures for all of the services.
		a Give the chart the heading: **SERVICES 2001**
		b Ensure that each segment is shaded in such a way that the data can be clearly identified (eg by pattern, colour or shade) when printed.
		c Each sector of the chart must be labelled clearly with the **service** and the **amount** or **percentage** of the spending.
5c	3	Save the pie chart.
5d	4	Print one copy of the pie chart.
		The second report will identify the spending on education for the last three years (1999 to 2001).
2c, 3c, 4a	5	Produce a bar chart showing the **EDUCATION** figures from **1999** to **2001**.
		a Display the year along the x axis
		b Set the y axis to display the range: **0 to 250**
		c Give the bar chart the heading: **EDUCATION SPENDING**
		d Label the x axis: **YEAR**
		e Label the y axis: **EXPENDITURE**
5c	6	Save the bar chart.
5d	7	Print one copy of the bar chart.

What You Have To Do

Assessment Objectives		
2b, 3b, 4a		The third report will identify the spending on both leisure and highways from 1997 to 2001.
	8	Produce a line graph comparing the data for **LEISURE** and **HIGHWAYS** from **1997** to **2001**.
		a Display the **years** along the x axis
		b Set the y axis to display the range: **15** to **45**
		c Give the graph the heading: **HIGHWAYS AND LEISURE EXPENDITURE**
		d Label the x axis: **YEAR**
		e Label the y axis: **SPENDING (£M)**
		f Use a legend to identify each line. Make sure that the lines and/or data points are distinctive, and can be identified when printed.
5c	9	Save the graph.
5d	10	Print one copy of the line graph.
5b	11	Save your data file.
5e	12	Close the document and exit the software securely.

Self-assessment: Task 5

Did I do it correctly?

- ☐ Opened an existing data document
- ☐ Used a pie chart
- ☐ Used a line graph
- ☐ Used a bar/column chart
- ☐ Selected a single data set
- ☐ Selected a comparative data set
- ☐ Selected a subset of a single data set
- ☐ Set axes' upper and lower limits
- ☐ Selected and displayed data labels
- ☐ Selected/entered headings and axes titles
- ☐ Used a legend
- ☐ Ensured that the comparative data was distinctive
- ☐ Saved the data document
- ☐ Saved the pie chart
- ☐ Saved the bar chart
- ☐ Saved the line graph
- ☐ Printed the pie chart
- ☐ Printed the bar chart
- ☐ Printed the line graph
- ☐ Closed the data document.

UNIT 8 Computer Art Overview

What is a computer art package?

Computer art applications allow you to design and draw your own designs, as well as using stored images to create artwork. The package will offer you a brush facility that will allow you to draw freely. You can build shapes with straight lines or use previously stored designs or outlines. You can import images and photographs. You can edit your design by changing the size or colour of items or filling areas with patterns, you can also move or turn shapes. Text can be added in a variety of fonts, sizes and styles.

Why use a computer art package?

Computer art applications allow you to do things that would be difficult, or even impossible, using traditional drawing techniques. Such computer applications will allow you to use computerised versions of paint brushes, rubbers, rulers and paint pots. You can store shapes and reproduce them in different sizes or at different angles. The computer system will allow you to save your work or part of a design and you can reload it at a later stage.

Computer art actions

The actual features of each package may vary but most packages are able to:

Import and place images

You can bring prepared pictures, images and photographs into your work. You can control the size and position required.

Create graphic shapes

You can draw your own shapes, some more common shapes like squares, oblongs, ellipses and circles are normally available. You can also load prepared shapes, drawings, images and designs.

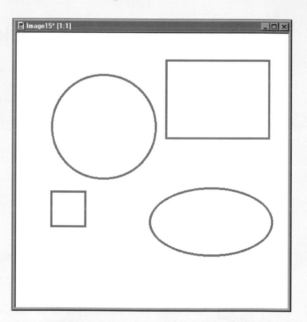

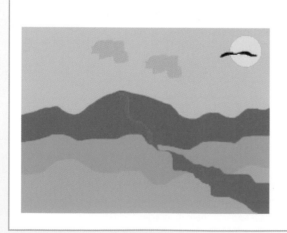

Samples of computer art

Change the size of items

You can control the size and position of any item. This function will allow you to increase or decrease the size of any part of your drawing.

Crop items

This facility will allow you to remove any part of an image that you do not require. You identify the area or part of your drawing you wish to crop and remove it.

Enter text

You will be able to control the size, style and font of the text you enter. Text is normally entered through the keyboard. You will also be able to amend the text and resize it if required.

Select colour

You can select a range of colours for any part of your design.

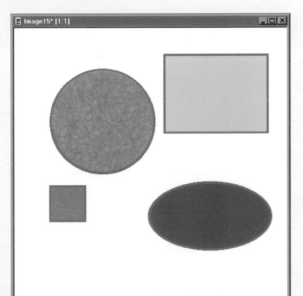

Rotate items

This will allow you to turn the position of the shape by a number of degrees.

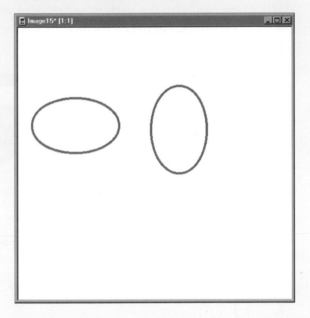

Flip items

This will allow you to 'flip' a shape along its horizontal or vertical axis.

Copy items

This facility will allow you to copy an item as many times as required. You identify the area or part of your drawing you wish to copy and paste it.

Delete an item

There is usually a facility to allow you to delete any part of the drawing, or you can delete the shapes. You will also be able to clear all the design.

Fill shapes

This will allow you to fill a shape, such as a square or circle or an enclosed part of a design, with the pattern or colour of your choice. Some packages refer to this facility as flood.

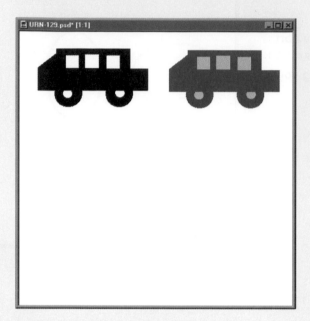

Select drawing instrument

The most common of these will be the brush, of which you can select the width of the line drawn. There is a wide variety of tools available.

Save

You can save your complete design or drawing and save individual shapes or sections of your design.

Print designs

The quality of the printing will be controlled by the quality of your printer. It is possible to use a full range of printers including colour, laser printers or a graphics plotter to produce your printout.

The options available are usually presented in the form of **Menus** and **Icons**.

Colours are selected from the **Palette**.

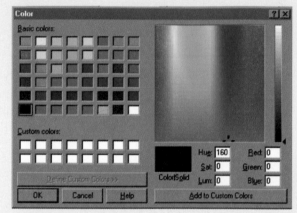

Helping you pass

Critical errors

- A missing or incorrect image.
- A missing block of text.

Accuracy errors

- Check the data you have entered as each **missing, incorrect or extra item of text** will count as a separate accuracy error.
- Check that you have completed all the objectives as each one not met will count as a separate error.

Tips

- Make sure you use the specified size for your artwork – there is a tolerance of 6 mm both horizontally and vertically on the printed size of your work.
- Make sure that the items in your artwork do not overlap.

Build Up Exercises

TASK 1

This task is designed to allow you to practise the skills required to gain OCR Level 1 Certificate for IT Users (NEW CLAIT) assessment objectives.

Before you begin

You will need to find out and note down how to:

- load your computer art application
- create a new document
- set artwork size/resolution
- import and place bitmapped image(s)
- crop an image
- resize an image to fit
- create a graphic shape
- use specified colours
- flip an item
- copy an item
- save a document
- print your artwork.

There is a checklist for you to complete on page 98 to use as a reference sheet.

You will need the image file **fish**.

You will find the **fish** file on the CD supplied with this book.

Scenario

You work as an administrator in an aquarium. You have been asked to produce a draft layout for a postcard to be sold in the gift shop. A rough sketch of the layout is given below:

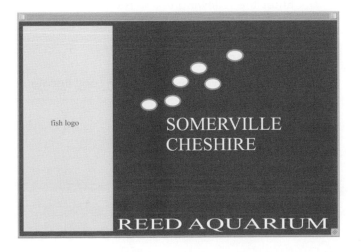

What You Have To Do

Assessment Objectives		
Ia, 5a, 5b	I	Using software that will allow you to create artwork, open a new document and set the size of the artwork to be 10 cm tall and 15 cm wide.
2a, 2b, 2c 4c, 4d	2	Import the image **FISH** and apply the following transformations:
		a Crop the image so that the first three fish are removed.
		b Flip the image horizontally so that the fish are now swimming to the left.
		c Place the image at the left edge of the artwork. Make sure that it is no wider than 4 cm.
2d, 4a	3	Draw a **blue** circle (bubble) as in the sketch. Copy the circle five times and arrange them in a similar manner to those shown in the sketch.
5c, 5e	4	Save the artwork and print one copy in colour.

TASK 2

This task is designed to allow you to practise the skills required to gain OCR Level 1 Certificate for IT Users (NEW CLAIT) assessment objectives.

Before you begin

You will need to find out and note down how to:

- enter text
- resize text to fit.

What You Have To Do

Assessment Objectives		
3a, 3c, 4a	I	Using the file created in Task 1, enter the following text in **red** along the bottom of the artwork:
		REED AQUARIUM
		Stretch this text to fit the full width from the right to the left edge of the artwork.
3a, 4a	2	Enter the following text in **red** in the clear space above the name of the aquarium, as shown in the sketch:
		SOMERVILLE
		CHESHIRE
5c, 5e	3	Save the artwork and print one copy in colour.

TASK 3

This task is designed to allow you to practise the skills required to gain OCR Level 1 Certificate for IT Users (NEW CLAIT) assessment objectives.

Before you begin

You will need to find out and note down how to:

- amend text
- rotate an item
- delete an item
- save a document with a new filename
- close a document.

What You Have To Do

Assessment Objectives		
3b, 3c 4b, 4e	1	Using the file created in Task 2, make these changes: **a** Delete the bubble closest to the fish. **b** Rotate the following text and place it down the right side of your artwork: **REED AQUARIUM** **c** Change the text **REED AQUARIUM** to become: **REED MANOR AQUARIUM** **d** Resize the amended text so that it is no wider than it was before the amendment. **e** Move the following text to the bottom edge of your artwork: **SOMERVILLE** **CHESHIRE**
5d, 5e	2	Make sure that none of the page items overlap. Save the artwork with a new filename and print one copy in colour.
1a, 5f	3	Close the document and exit the software securely.

Computer Art Checklist

You should complete this checklist for each hardware and software combination you use. Use information from your tutor, handouts, handbooks and software manuals to complete the list. You can then use your list as a reference sheet to complete the practice tasks that follow.

Hardware: _____

Software: _____

ASSESSMENT OBJECTIVE	HOW TO DO IT	OCR REFERENCE
1 Identify and use appropriate software correctly		
Use appropriate application software	_____	1a
2 Import, crop and resize images		
Import and place bitmapped image(s)	_____	2a
Crop image	_____	2b
Resize image(s) to fit	_____	2c
Create graphic shape(s)	_____	2d
3 Enter, amend and resize text		
Enter text	_____	3a
Amend text	_____	3b
Resize text to fit	_____	3c
4 Manipulate and format page items		
Use specified colours	_____	4a
Rotate item	_____	4b
Flip item	_____	4c
Copy item	_____	4d
Delete item	_____	4e
5 Manage and print artwork		
Create new document	_____	5a
Save artwork size/resolution	_____	5b
Save document	_____	5c
Save document with new filename	_____	5d
Print artwork	_____	5e
Close document	_____	5f

OCR Assignments and Self-Assessments

This task allows you to practise a complete OCR Level 1 Certificate for IT Users (NEW CLAIT) assignment. It covers all the OCR Level 1 Certificate for IT Users (NEW CLAIT) computer art assessment objectives.

You will need the image files **DISKS** and **DEEDEE**.

You will find the **DISKS** and **DEEDEE** files on the CD supplied with this book.

Scenario

You work as an administrator for a company that produces disks for use in a variety of manufacturing processes. You have been asked to produce a draft layout for a display at a forthcoming trade show. A rough sketch of the layout is given below:

What You Have To Do

Assessment Objectives		
1a, 5a, 5b	1	Using software that will allow you to create artwork, open a new document and set the size of the artwork to be 10 cm tall and 12 cm wide.
2a, 2b, 2c	2	Import the image **DISKS** and apply the following transformations: **a** Crop the image to remove the three disks at the bottom. **b** Place the image in the top right corner of the artwork. **c** Resize the image in proportion so that it does not extend below the centre point down the artwork.
2a, 2c, 4c	3	Import the image **DEEDEE** and apply the following transformations: **a** Flip the image horizontally so that the straight lines are on the left. **b** Place the image in the top left corner of the artwork. **c** Resize the image in proportion so that it does not take up more than 2.5 cm square space.
2d, 4a	4	Draw a thick **red** line across the middle of your artwork.
2d, 4a	5	Draw a small rectangle (approximately 2.5 cm tall by 1.5 cm wide) in the bottom left corner of the artwork. Use a **black** edge.
4d	6	Copy the rectangle twice, placing the copies alongside the original and spacing them across the artwork, as shown on the layout sketch.
4a	7	Colour the rectangles as follows: left rectangle: **black** middle rectangle: **red** right rectangle: **black**
3a, 4a	8	Enter the following text in **black** in a clear space at the top of the artwork, on two lines as shown: **DOME** **DISKS**
3a, 3c, 4a	9	Enter the following text in **red** in the clear space below the red line and above the rectangles: **DIAMOND RELIABILITY** **LIFE GUARANTEE** Stretch this text to fit the full width from the right to the left edge of the artwork.
5c, 5e	10	Save the artwork and print one copy in colour.
3b, 4a, 4e	11	Your manager has requested some changes: **a** Delete the text: **DIAMOND RELIABILITY** **b** Change the text **LIFE GUARANTEE** to become: **LIFETIME GUARANTEE** **c** Change the colour of the text **LIFETIME GUARANTEE** to **red**.
4b	12	Rotate all the rectangles **90 degrees clockwise**. If necessary, resize to fit between the left and right sides of the artwork without overlapping.
5d, 5e	13	Make sure that none of the page items overlap. Save the artwork with a new filename and print one copy in colour.
1a, 5f	14	Close the document and exit the software securely.

Self-assessment: Task 4

Did I do it correctly?

☐ Using appropriate application software opened a new document and set the size of the artwork to be 10 cm tall and 12 cm wide

☐ Imported the image **DISKS** and:
- cropped the image to remove the 3 disks at the bottom
- placed the image in the top right corner
- resized the image in proportion so that it did not extend below the centre

☐ Imported the image **DEEDEE** and:
- flipped the image horizontally
- placed the image in the top left corner of the artwork
- resized the image in proportion so that it takes up no more than 2.5 cm square space

☐ Drew a thick **red** line across the middle of your artwork

☐ Drew a small rectangle (approximately 2.5 cm tall by 1.5 cm wide) in the bottom left corner, using a **black** edge.

☐ Copied the rectangle twice, placing the copies alongside the original and spacing them across the artwork

☐ Coloured the left rectangle **black,** the middle rectangle **red,** and the right rectangle **black**

☐ Entered **DOME DISKS** in **black** at the top of the artwork, on **two** lines

☐ Entered **DIAMOND RELIABILITY LIFE GUARANTEE** in **red** below the red line and above the rectangles, and stretched it to fit the full width from the right to the left edge

☐ Deleted the text **DIAMOND RELIABILITY**

☐ Changed the text **LIFE GUARANTEE** to **LIFETIME GUARANTEE**

☐ Changed the colour of the text **LIFETIME GUARANTEE** to **red**

☐ Rotated all the rectangles **90 degrees clockwise** without overlapping them

☐ Saved the artwork

☐ Saved the artwork with a new filename

☐ Printed your work in colour

☐ Closed your work and exited the application software

TASK 5

This task allows you to practise a complete OCR Level 1 Certificate for IT Users (NEW CLAIT) assignment. It covers all the OCR Level 1 Certificate for IT Users (NEW CLAIT) computer art assessment objectives.

You will need the image files **HAT** and **IVY**.

You will find the **HAT** and **IVY** files on the CD supplied with this book.

Scenario

You work as an administrator for a company that produces millinery items and accessories. You have been asked to produce a draft layout for one of the retail outlets in the group. A rough sketch of the layout is given on the next page:

What You Have To Do

Assessment Objectives		
1a, 5a, 5b	1	Using software that will allow you to create artwork, open a new document and set the size of the artwork to be 10 cm tall and 10 cm wide.
2a, 2b, 2c 4c	2	Import the image **HAT** and apply the following transformations: **a** Crop the image so that only the ellipse containing the lady wearing the hat remains. **b** Place the image in the top right corner of the artwork. **c** Resize the image in proportion so that it is approximately 4.5 cm tall and 3.5 cm wide. **d** Flip the image horizontally so that the lady is now facing to the left.
2a, 2c, 4b	3	Import the image **IVY** and apply the following transformations: **a** Rotate the image **90 degrees**. **b** Place the image in the top left corner of the artwork. **c** Resize the image to fit between the top and bottom of the artwork.

2d, 4a	4	Draw a thick **black** line across the middle of your artwork.
3a, 4a	5	Enter the following text in **black** in a clear space at the top of the artwork, on two lines as shown on the sketch:

HAUGHTY

HATS

3a, 3c, 4a	6	Enter the following text in **red** in the clear space below the black line:

BAGS

GLOVES

ACCESSORIES

PARAPHERNALIA

Stretch this text to fit the full width from the ivy on the left to the right edge of the artwork.

5c, 5e	7	Save the artwork and print one copy in colour.
2d, 3b, 3c	8	Your manager has requested some changes:
4a, 4e		

    a   Delete the image **IVY**.

    b   Remove **GLOVES** from the text. Stretch the remainder of the text to fit the full width of your artwork.

    c   Change the colour of the following text to **blue**:

        BAGS

        ACCESSORIES

        PARAPHERNALIA

    d   Using point size 10, change the **edge** of the black line using the 'photo brush' to daisies (or suitable alternative, eg ivy).

    e   Extend the line from the left to the right edge of the artwork.

4d	9	Copy the line to the bottom of the artwork.
5d, 5e	10	Make sure that none of the page items overlap. Save the artwork with a new filename and print one copy in colour.
5f	11	Close the document and exit the software securely.

Self-assessment: Task 5

Did I do it correctly?

- [ ] Used appropriate application software
- [ ] Imported and placed a bitmapped image(s)
- [ ] Cropped the image
- [ ] Resized the image(s) to fit
- [ ] Created graphic shape(s)
- [ ] Entered text
- [ ] Amended text
- [ ] Used specified colours
- [ ] Rotated an item and flipped an item
- [ ] Copied an item and deleted an item
- [ ] Created a new document
- [ ] Set artwork size/resolution
- [ ] Saved a document
- [ ] Saved a document with a new filename
- [ ] Printed artwork
- [ ] Closed a document.

UNIT 9 Web Pages Overview

What is web page creation software?

It is a package that allows you to create, link and format web pages. It allows you to create web pages to permit navigation of your site and use of hyperlinks to take you to other pages in your site, to pages on other sites, or to e-mail addresses. It also allows you to print the work that you create.

Why use web page creation software?

Using web page creation software allows you to create your own web pages and to link them to other relevant areas to give information about your company or your products and services.

The software will allow you to use text and images to make your site both useful and interesting.

Web sites are usually based on menus using a homepage that leads to sub-menus that lead to information. A menu choice can be represented as a word or an image.

When you are planning web pages you should consider:

- what you trying to achieve – what you want to get out of the site
- your users – the people who are going to visit the site
- the information – the content and what it offers.

Attracting visitors and encouraging their frequent return is the goal of most web sites. You can't deliver a message without an audience. There are many methods for attracting visitors but you should aim to incorporate dynamic content into your pages to increase the interest level.

An example of a web homepage

General

The Internet carries an enormous range of materials and you may want to use it to share your ideas or promote an activity.

It enables people from around the world to view your web pages, and in doing so allows you access to data, information and people that may otherwise be outside of your scope.

When people go on the Internet they may have a specific destination in mind, or they may wish to browse through the Web looking for topics or things of interest.

If you want them to visit, and return to your web site, then it has to generate sufficient interest to produce this result.

Input

You can enter text from the keyboard or load it from prepared text files. You can also incorporate images and photographs.

Processing

Your computer program will manipulate the text and images into HTML code so that it is usable as a web page.

Output

If you want to print the pages you have created you can do this in two ways:

- as you see it on the screen
- as HTML code.

You will find that the vocabulary of the Internet and web pages is taken from sources familiar to us:

- from travel: superhighway, engine, cruising, surfing, navigating
- from restaurants: menu, server
- from words used for medieval manuscripts: icon, scroll and cursor.

Web page terms

Hyperlinks

Most sites include hyperlinks. A hyperlink is a way of getting from one page to another destination without having to enter the address.

You may move to a different location on the same page (a picture, an e-mail address or a program). You may also move to a new page on your own web or to:

- **a new page** – you must enter the link to take you to the specified destination.
- **a page or file on the WWW** – you can add a link to a page that is not in your web (an external link). It may take you to a search page or to another site's home page.
- **send an e-mail message** – the link will open and address an e-mail message to the address you specify – eg, if you want visitors to send you feedback you can create a link that creates an e-mail message addressed to your e-mail alias.

Link text

This is the text that you highlight to use as the link from the origin to the destination.

HTML

Hypertext markup language describes the contents and appearance of elements on a page, such as paragraph, table, or image.

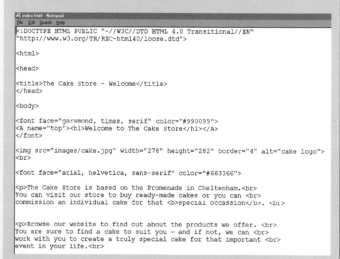

```
index.html - Notepad
File  Edit  Search  Help
<!DOCTYPE HTML PUBLIC "-//W3C//DTD HTML 4.0 Transitional//EN"
"http://www.w3.org/TR/REC-html40/loose.dtd">

<html>

<head>

<title>The Cake Store - Welcome</title>
</head>

<body>

<font face="garamond, times, serif" color="#990099">
<A name="top"><h1>Welcome to The Cake Store</h1></A>
</font>

<img src="images/cake.jpg" width="278" height="282" border="4" alt="cake logo">
<br>

<font face="arial, helvetica, sans-serif" color="#663366">

<p>The Cake Store is based on the Promenade in Cheltenham.<br>
You can visit our store to buy ready-made cakes or you can <br>
commission an individual cake for that <b>special occassion</b>. <br>


<p>Browse our website to find out about the products we offer. <br>
You are sure to find a cake to suit you – and if not, we can <br>
work with you to create a truly special cake for that important <br>
event in your life.<br>
```

GIF files

Images that can add a dynamic element, promote specific information and events, and highlight navigation.

URL

To get to a site you enter an Internet address in the space provided on the browser. Web addresses, sometimes called uniform resource locators (URLs), begin with http:// – hypertext transfer protocol.

Navigation

After you enter the web address, the site's homepage will appear. You will then have more choices to take you further into the site.

Align

You can align your text and images to the left, centre or right.

Helping you pass

Critical errors

- A link that does not load the correct page.
- A link that does not generate the correct address for an e-mail message.
- A missing image.

Accuracy errors

- Check the data you have entered as each **missing, incorrect or extra character** will count as a separate accuracy error. A line of linked text counts as one accuracy error only. The imported text is not assessed for accuracy.
- Check that you have completed all the objectives as each one not met will count as a separate error.

Tips

- Check and test your links carefully as any link that fails to load the correct page is a critical error.

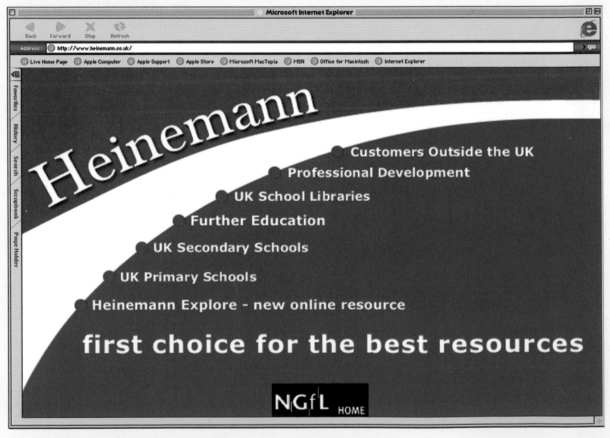

A web site home page showing contents

Build Up Exercises

TASK 1

This task is designed to allow you to practise the skills required to gain OCR Level 1 Certificate for IT Users (NEW CLAIT) assessment objectives.

Before you begin

You will need to find out and note down how to:

- load an appropriate application to produce web pages
- link pages
- test links
- save a document
- edit text.

There is a checklist for you to complete on page 111 to use as a reference sheet.

In Tasks 1 to 3 you will need access to:

- an unlinked set of HTML formatted pages: **courses.htm** and **times.htm**
- these pages require the graphic file: **bradlogo.gif**
- the graphic file: **college.gif**
- the text file: **sites.txt**

All these files are on the CD supplied with this book.

Scenario

You are working as an administrator for Progress College. Your duties include the preparation of web pages.

What You Have To Do

Assessment Objectives		
1a, 3e, 4a 5b	1	Load application software that will allow you to create web pages. Two unlinked pages have been prepared that have to be linked. They are: • **courses.htm**, the 'COURSES' homepage • **times.htm**, a page with course time details. Create a link in the **courses.htm** page as follows: Text to be linked: **Times** Link to: **times.htm** Enter your name and centre number after the text: **Updated by**: Save the amended **courses.htm** page.

What You Have To Do

Assessment Objectives		
3e, 4a	2	Create a link in the **times.htm** page as follows: Text to be linked: **Courses** Link to: **courses.htm** Enter your name and centre number after the text: **Updated by:** Save the amended **times.htm** page. **It is important that you check that the links are correct before proceeding further.**
4d	3	Reload each page in the browser and test that the links function correctly.

TASK 2

This task is designed to allow you to practise the skills required to gain OCR Level 1 Certificate for IT Users (NEW CLAIT) assessment objectives.

Before you begin

You will need to find out and note down how to:

- create a new document
- insert and place an image and insert a text file
- use 3 different font sizes
- control text flow
- align page items
- emphasise text
- insert link text
- retain original data and formatting.

What You Have To Do

Assessment Objectives		
2a, 3e, 5a	1	You have been asked to make a new page displaying the sites. An outline of the page is shown below:

```
bradlogo.gif

college.gif

SITES
DAYTIME COURSES
Todbridge Adult Education Centre
EVENING COURSES
Hopgate End Community School
Todbridge Adult Education Centre
COURSES

_____
Updated by:
```

Create a new document and insert the text file **sites.txt**.

Enter your name and centre number after the text: **Updated by:**

What You Have To Do

Assessment Objectives		
3b, 3f	2	The new page must be formatted according to the college's web design policy as shown in the diagram.
		Format the text **SITES** as a heading (large font size).
		Format the text **DAYTIME COURSES** and **EVENING COURSES** as subheadings (medium font size).
		Format all other text as body text (small font size).
		Ensure that each of the lines is separated by a clear line space.
3a, 3d	3	Format all the text above the line to be centre-aligned on the page.
		Format the text **Updated by**: to be left-aligned on the page.
		Embolden the text **SITES**.
		Italicise the text *DAYTIME COURSES* and *EVENING COURSES*.
2b, 3a	4	The page must include the college logo.
		Import the image **bradlogo.gif** and position it at the top of the page.
2b, 3a	5	The page must include the graphic of a college.
		Import the graphic **college.gif** and place it below the logo and above the text **SITES**.
		Make sure that the graphic is centre-aligned on the page.
4a, 5b	6	The new page should link back to the '**COURSES**' homepage. Create a link in the new page as follows:
		Text to be linked: **COURSES**
		Link to: **courses.htm**
		Save the new page as **sites.htm**.
3a, 4a, 4e 4f, 5b	7	The 'COURSES' page should have a link to the new page. In the **courses.htm** page, on a separate line below the text **TIMES** and above the text **Updated by**:, add the text: **SITES**
		Format this text to be centre-aligned on the page.
		Link this text to your newly created page.
		Save the amended **courses.htm** page.
4d	8	Load all the pages into the browser and test the new links.

TASK **3**

This task is designed to allow you to practise the skills required to gain OCR Level 1 Certificate for IT Users (NEW CLAIT) assessment objectives.

Before you begin

You will need to find out and note down how to:

- change background colour
- insert external link
- insert e-mail link
- print web pages
- print HTML source code
- close a document.

What You Have To Do

Assessment Objectives		
3c, 5b	1	A different background colour will improve the 'COURSES' homepage. Change the background colour of the **courses.htm** page ensuring that it is different from the text colour. Save the amended **courses.htm** page.
4b, 4f, 5b	2	Some of the links on the 'COURSES' homepage have not been completed. Create an external link in the **courses.htm** page as follows: Text to be linked: **COLLEGE HOME PAGE** External link to: **www.progress-media.co.uk** Save the amended **courses.htm** page.
4c, 4f, 5b	3	Create an e-mail link in the **courses.htm** page as follows: Text to be linked: **Your name and centre number** External link to: **enquiries@progress-media.co.uk** Save the amended **courses.htm** page.
5c, 5d	4	Carry out the following tasks to show the amendments you have made: **a** Load the **courses.htm** page into the browser and print a copy. **b** Load the **times.htm** page into the browser and print a copy. **c** Load the **sites.htm** page into the browser and print a copy. **d** Print a copy of the HTML code used for each of the 3 pages.
1a, 5e	5	Close each document and exit from the software you are using following the correct procedures.

Web Pages Checklist

You should complete this checklist for each hardware and software combination you use. Use information from your tutor, handouts, handbooks and software manuals to complete the list. You can then use your list as a reference sheet to complete the practice tasks that follow.

Hardware: _____

Software: _____

ASSESSMENT OBJECTIVE	HOW TO DO IT	OCR REFERENCE
1 Identify and use appropriate software correctly		
Use appropriate application software	_____	la
2 Import and place text and image files		
Insert text file	_____	2a
Insert and place image	_____	2b
3 Amend and format web pages		
Align page items	_____	3a
Use 3 different font sizes	_____	3b
Change background colour	_____	3c
Emphasise text	_____	3d
Edit text	_____	3e
Control text flow	_____	3f
4 Insert relative, external and e-mail hyperlinks		
Link pages	_____	4a
Insert external link	_____	4b
Insert e-mail link	_____	4c
Test links	_____	4d
Insert link text	_____	4e
Retain original data and formatting	_____	4f
5 Manage and print web pages		
Create new document	_____	5a
Save document	_____	5b
Print web pages	_____	5c
Print HTML source code	_____	5d
Close document	_____	5e

OCR Assignments and Self-Assessments

TASK 4

This task allows you to practise a complete OCR Level 1 Certificate for IT Users (NEW CLAIT) assignment. It covers all the OCR Level 1 Certificate for IT Users (NEW CLAIT) web pages assessment objectives.

In this task you will need access to:

- an unlinked set of HTML formatted pages:
  location.htm
  facilities.htm
- which require the graphic file:
  hotlogo.gif

- the graphic file:
  bang.gif
- the text file:
  events.txt

All these files are on the CD supplied with this book.

Scenario

You are working as an administrator for the Progress Hotel Group. Your duties include the preparation of web pages.

What You Have To Do

Assessment Objectives		
1a, 3e, 4a 5b	1	Load application software that will allow you to create web pages. Two unlinked pages have been prepared that have to be linked. They are: • **location.htm**, the 'LOCATION' homepage • **facilities.htm**, a page showing the facilities at the hotel. Create a link in the **location.htm** page as follows: Text to be linked:　**Facilities** Link to:　　　　　**facilities.htm** Enter your name and centre number after the text: **Updated by:** Save the amended **location.htm** page.
3e, 4a	2	Create a link in the **facilities.htm** page as follows: Text to be linked:　**Location** Link to:　　　　　**location.htm** Enter your name and centre number after the text: **Updated by:** Save the amended **facilities.htm** page. **It is important that you check that the links are correct before proceeding further.**

What You Have To Do

Assessment Objectives		
4d	3	Reload each page in the browser and test that the links function correctly.
2a, 3e, 5a	4	You have been asked to make a new page displaying forthcoming events. An outline of the page is shown below:

hotlogo.gif

FORTHCOMING EVENTS

DECEMBER

10th   City Transport and Communications Conference
12th   International Relief Conference

bang.gif

21st   Progress Group Christmas Ball
25th   Christmas Banquet

Updated by:

		Create a new document and insert the text file **events.txt**.
		Enter your name and centre number after the text: **Updated by**:
3b, 3f	5	The new page must be formatted according to the company's web design policy as shown in the diagram above.
		Format the text **FORTHCOMING EVENTS** as a heading (large font size).
		Format the text **DECEMBER** as a subheading (medium font size).
		Format all other text as body text (small font size).
		Ensure that each of the lines is separated by a clear line space.
3a, 3d	6	Format all the text above the line to be centre-aligned on the page.
		Format the text **Updated by**: to be left-aligned on the page.
		Embolden the text **25th Christmas Banquet**.
		Italicise the text *DECEMBER*.
2b, 3a	7	The page must include the hotel logo.
		Import the image **hotlogo.gif** and position it at the top of the page.
2b, 3a	8	The page must include the 'celebration' graphic.
		Import the graphic **bang.gif** and place it below the text **12th International Relief Conference** and above the text **21st Progress Group Christmas Ball**.
		Make sure that the graphic is centre-aligned on the page.
4a, 5b	9	The new page should link back to the 'LOCATION' homepage. Create a link in the new page as follows:
		Text to be linked: **Location**
		Link to: **location.htm**
		Save the new page as **events.htm**.
3a, 4a, 4e 4f, 5b	10	The 'LOCATION' page should have a link to the new page. In the **location.htm** page, on a separate line below the text **Facilities** and above the text **Updated by**:, add the text: **Events**
		Format this text to be centre-aligned on the page.
		Link this text to your newly created page.
		Save the amended **location.htm** page.
4d	11	Load all the pages into the browser and test the new links.
3c, 5b	12	A different background colour will improve the 'LOCATION' homepage. Change the background colour of the **location.htm** page ensuring that it is different from the text colour.
		Save the amended **location.htm** page.

4b, 4f, 5b	13	Some of the links on the 'LOCATION' homepage have not been completed. Create an external link in the **location.htm** page as follows:

Text to be linked:　**Progress Group Home Page**
External link to:　www.progress-media.co.uk
Save the amended **location.htm** page.

4c, 4f, 5b	14	Create an e-mail link in the **location.htm** page as follows:

Text to be linked:　**Your name and centre number**
External link to:　enquiries@progress-media.co.uk
Save the amended **location.htm** page.

5c, 5d	15	Carry out the following tasks to show the amendments you have made:

 a Load the **location.htm** page into the browser and print a copy.
 b Load the **facilities.htm** page into the browser and print a copy.
 c Load the **events.htm** page into the browser and print a copy.
 d Print a copy of the HTML code used for each of the 3 pages.

1a, 5e	16	Close each document and exit from the software you are using following the correct procedures.

Self-assessment: Task 4

Did I do it correctly?

- ☐ Loaded application software to create web pages
- ☐ Created a link on **Facilities** in the **location.htm** page to **facilities.htm** and a link on **Location** in the **facilities.htm** page to **location.htm** and entered your name and centre number after the text: **Updated by:** on both pages
- ☐ Created a new document and:
  - • inserted the text file **events.txt**
  - • entered your name and centre number after the text: **Updated by:**
  - • imported the image:
    - • **hotlogo.gif** and placed it at the top of the page
    - • **bang.gif** and placed it below **12th International Relief Conference** and above **21st Progress Group Christmas Ball**
- ☐ Formatted your new document as follows:
  - • **FORTHCOMING EVENTS** as a heading (large font size)
  - • **DECEMBER** as a subheading (medium font size)
  - • all other text as body text (small font size)
  - • placed a clear line space between each of the lines of text
  - • centred the text and graphics

- • left aligned the text **Updated by:**
- • emboldened the text **25th Christmas Banquet** and italicised the text *DECEMBER*
- ☐ Saved the new page as **events.htm** and created a link on **Location** to **location.htm**
- ☐ Added text and linked the new text **Events** in the **location.htm** page to your newly created page
- ☐ Changed the background colour of the **location.htm** page
- ☐ Created an external link on **Progress Group Home Page** in the **location.htm** page to **www.progress-media.co.uk**
- ☐ Created an e-mail link on **Your name and centre number** in the **location.htm** page to enquiries@progress-media.co.uk
- ☐ Saved the amended pages: **location.htm** and **facilities.htm**
- ☐ Loaded pages into the browser to check links and to display amendments
- ☐ Printed the pages: **location.htm; facilities.htm; events.htm,** plus a copy of the HTML code used for each of the 3 pages
- ☐ Closed each document and exited from the software

TASK 5

This task allows you to practise a complete OCR Level 1 Certificate for IT Users (NEW CLAIT) assignment. It covers all the OCR Level 1 Certificate for IT Users (NEW CLAIT) web pages assessment objectives.

In this task you will need access to:

- an unlinked set of HTML formatted pages:
  locations.htm
  prices.htm
- which require the graphic file:
  phlogo.gif
- the graphic file:
  skyline.gif
- the text file:
  newdevs.txt

All these files are on the CD supplied with this book.

Scenario

You are working as an administrator for the Progress Housing Group. Your duties include the preparation of web pages.

	What You Have To Do	
Assessment Objectives		
1a, 3e, 4a 5b	1	Load application software that will allow you to create web pages. Two unlinked pages have been prepared that have to be linked. They are: • **locations.htm**, the 'LOCATIONS' homepage • **prices.htm**, a page showing the house prices Create a link in the **locations.htm** page as follows: Text to be linked: **Prices** Link to: **prices.htm**. Enter your name and centre number after the text: **Updated by**: Save the amended **locations.htm** page.
3e, 4a	2	Create a link in the **prices.htm** page as follows: Text to be linked: **Locations** Link to: **locations.htm**. Enter your name and centre number after the text: **Updated by**: Save the amended **prices.htm** page. **It is important that you check that the links are correct before proceeding further.**
4d	3	Reload each page in the browser and test that the links function correctly.

What You Have To Do

Assessment Objectives		
2a, 3e, 5a	4	You have been asked to make a new page displaying details of a new development in South Manchester. An outline of the page is shown below: Create a new document and insert the text file **newdevs.txt**. Enter your name and centre number after the text: **Updated by**:

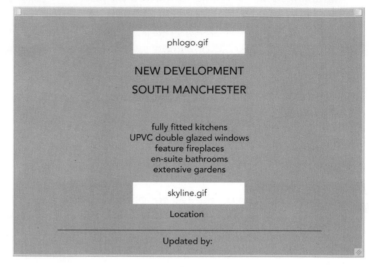

3b, 3f	5	The new page must be formatted according to the company's web design policy as shown in the diagram above.

Format the text **NEW DEVELOPMENT** as a heading (large font size).

Format the text **SOUTH MANCHESTER** as a subheading (medium font size).

Format all other text as body text (small font size).

Ensure that each of the lines is separated by a clear line space.

3a, 3d	6	Format all the text to be centre-aligned on the page.

Embolden and italicise the text **SOUTH MANCHESTER**.

2b, 3a	7	The page must include the company logo.

Import the image **phlogo.gif** and position it at the top of the page.

2b, 3a	8	The page must include the graphic showing a typical skyline.

Import the graphic **skyline.gif** and place it below the text **extensive gardens** and above the text **Location**.

Make sure that the graphic is centre-aligned on the page.

4a, 5b	9	The new page should link back to the 'LOCATIONS' homepage. Create a link in the new page as follows: Text to be linked: **Locations** Link to: **locations.htm**

Save the new page as **newdevs.htm**.

3a, 4a, 4e 4f, 5b	10	The 'LOCATIONS' page should have a link to the new page. In the **locations.htm** page, on a separate line below the text **Prices** and above the text **Updated by**:, add the text: **New Development**

Format this text to be centre-aligned on the page.

Link this text to your newly created page.

Save the amended **locations.htm** page.

4d	11	Load all the pages into the browser and test the new links.

What You Have To Do

Assessment Objectives		
3c, 5b	12	A different background colour will improve the 'LOCATIONS' homepage. Change the background colour of the **locations.htm** page ensuring that it is different from the text colour.
		Save the amended **locations.htm** page.
4b, 4f, 5b	13	Some of the links on the 'LOCATIONS' homepage have not been completed. Create an external link in the **locations.htm** page as follows:
		Text to be linked: **Progress Group Home Page**
		External link to: **www.progress-media.co.uk**
		Save the amended **locations.htm** page.
4c, 4f, 5b	14	Create an e-mail link in the **locations.htm** page as follows:
		Text to be linked: **Your name and centre number**
		External link to: **enquiries@progress-media.co.uk**
		Save the amended **locations.htm** page.
5c, 5d	15	Carry out the following tasks to show the amendments you have made:
		a Load the **locations.htm** page into the browser and print a copy.
		b Load the **prices.htm** page into the browser and print a copy.
		c Load the **newdevs.htm** page into the browser and print a copy.
		d Print a copy of the HTML code used for each of the 3 pages.
1a, 5e	16	Close each document and exit from the software you are using following the correct procedures.

Self-assessment: Task 5

Did I do it correctly?

- [ ] Used appropriate application software
- [ ] Inserted the text file
- [ ] Inserted and placed the image
- [ ] Aligned page items as specified
- [ ] Used 3 different font sizes as specified
- [ ] Changed the background colour as specified
- [ ] Emphasised text as specified
- [ ] Edited text as specified
- [ ] Controlled text flow
- [ ] Linked pages

- [ ] Inserted an external link
- [ ] Inserted an e-mail link
- [ ] Tested the links
- [ ] Inserted link text
- [ ] Retained original data and formatting
- [ ] Created a new document
- [ ] Saved documents
- [ ] Printed web pages
- [ ] Printed the HTML source code
- [ ] Closed documents.

UNIT 10

Presentation Graphics Overview

What is a presentation graphics package?

Presentation graphics applications allow you to set up slides and slide shows to make your presentations more dynamic and interesting.

You can incorporate prepared text and images to create presentations.

Some packages offer you a variety of templates and pre-prepared presentations for you to add your own text and graphics.

You should be able to format the background (colour), the text (font and size) and manipulate the image in terms of size and position.

Why use a presentation graphics package?

Presentation graphics applications allow you to prepare presentations and present your information using a variety of styles and techniques that would not otherwise be available.

As well as being able to provide a copy of your presentation for your audience (to enable them, say, to make notes, and take away at the end of the presentation) you can provide an interesting and dynamic presentation of slides.

Presentations can also be set to run automatically so that there is no need for intervention. This may be used, for example, at an exhibition to provide information to visitors on events taking place at the exhibition, or forthcoming events.

Input

You can enter text from the keyboard or import it from file. You will be able to control the font, font size, style and format of the text you enter. You can also import graphics, images, charts, etc.

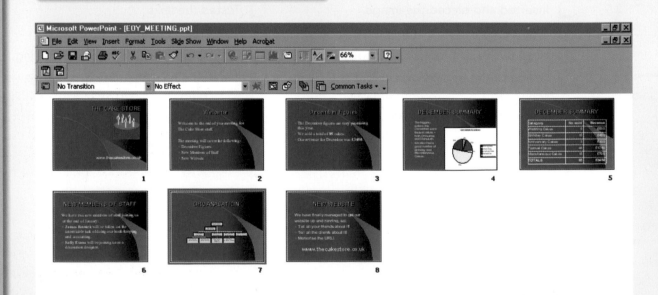

An example of a PowerPoint presentation

Output

Printing

When printing your presentation the quality will be controlled by the quality of your printer.

You can print your entire presentation – the slides, outline, notes and audience handouts. You can also print specific slides, handouts, notes pages or outline pages.

You can print all the text in your outline or just the slide titles. Formatting can be 'hidden' on screen but will always be shown on printouts.

You can make overhead transparencies from your slides and create 35 mm slides.

When you print audience handouts you can select from different layouts – they vary the number of slides, and orientation.

Running your presentation

As well as printing your presentation you will have the facility to run the presentation on your computer.

You can 'rehearse' the running of your presentation so that you can add any additional features for interest.

Presentation graphics actions

The features of each package may vary but most packages are able to:

Apply design templates

The templates contain colour schemes and custom formatting that will be applied to any slides you prepare in that presentation.

Create your own slide style

You can create your own style for your presentation. Once the frames are selected you can enter text from the keyboard or import it from file, images or charts.

Master slide

This is created so that all the slides in the presentation look the same.

Change graphic size and position

You should be able to increase or decrease the size of a graphic. You can also mark and drag the graphic to any position on the slide.

Select background colour

This will be the colour or pattern onto which you place your slide material.

Formatting

You can select the font you wish to use and also the size of the font.

There will also be facilities to allow:

- Bullets
- Alignment (left, centre and right)
- Enhancement (such as bold or italics)
- Replacement of text – ie replacing one word or 'string' for another.

Setting presentation features

You should be able to set up features in your presentation, including the manner in which the slides appear on the screen, the length of time they remain on the screen, and the manner in which you move to the next slide.

Helping you pass

Critical errors
- A missing image.
- An missing slide.

Accuracy errors
- Check the data that you have entered as **each line of text that has a missing, incorrect or extra word** will count as a separate accuracy error.
- Check that you have completed all the objectives as each one not met will count as a separate error.

Tips
- Make sure you create a master page as you will be penalised if the slide layout is inconsistent on the slides. Font sizes must also be consistent on the slides.
- Bullets must only be used where specified.

Build Up Exercises

This task is designed to allow you to practise the skills required to gain OCR Level 1 Certificate for IT Users (NEW CLAIT) assessment objectives.

Before you begin

You will need to find out and note down how to:

- load your presentation graphics application
- create a new presentation
- create text areas/text frames
- apply background
- insert graphic
- use specified font sizes
- use bullets
- apply alignment and enhancement
- insert text
- save a document.

There is a checklist for you to complete on page 123 to use as a reference sheet.

You will need the image file **butlogo** which is on the CD supplied with this book.

Scenario

You work as an administrator for a company that runs exhibitions. You have been asked to produce a slide show presentation to inform visitors about the cookery displays that will be taking place during the day.

What You Have To Do

Assessment Objectives		**You have been asked to produce a short presentation of 3 slides.**
1a	1	Load application software to allow you to produce a slide show presentation.
2a, 2b, 2c	2	Create a master slide as follows:
3a, 3b, 3c		a Create a page-wide **title** frame at the top of the page.
3d, 4b, 4e		b Create a page-wide **main** frame below the title frame.
5a		c Set up the text styles in these frames as follows:

Frame	Style	Emphasis	Size	Bullets	Alignment
title	title	bold only	54	no	centre
main	1st level	none	24	yes	left
main	2nd level	italic only	20	yes	left and indented

What You Have To Do

Assessment Objectives		
	d	Place the image **butlogo** at the bottom right corner of the slide. Make sure that the image does not overlap the text frames.
	e	Create a frame at the bottom of the page, below the main frame. Enter your name, centre number and today's date in this frame.
	f	Format the background to be white.
5b	3	Save the master slide. This master slide is to be used for all 3 slides.

TASK 2

This task is designed to allow you to practise the skills required to gain OCR Level 1 Certificate for IT Users (NEW CLAIT) assessment objectives.

Before you begin

You will need to find out and note down how to:

- insert text
- print slides.

What You Have To Do

The master slide is to be used for all 3 slides.

Assessment Objectives		
4a, 4b	1	Create slide 1 and enter the title: **COOKERY DISPLAYS**
		Leave the main frame blank for this slide.
4a, 4b	2	Create slide 2 and enter the title: **SNACKS**

Enter the following text in the main frame, with the styles shown:

ARTICHOKE AND CHEESE PUFFS	1st level
POLENTA BISCUITS WITH ONION SALSA	1st level
SESAME ROUNDS	1st level
TOMATO AND ROSEMARY BISCOTTI	1st level
TARTINES	1st level
ANCHOIADA	1st level

Assessment Objectives		
4a, 4b	3	Create slide 3 and enter the title: **LUNCH AND DINNER**

Enter the following text in the main frame, with the styles shown:

LUNCH	1st level
TOMATO AND CHICK PEA SOUP	2nd level
GREEN MANGO SALAD	2nd level
CHICKEN, PEANUT AND NOODLE SOUP	2nd level
GARLIC AND ROSEMARY FOCCACIA	2nd level
DINNER	1st level
CURRY ONION NOODLES WITH EGG	2nd level
SABJI ONION CURRY	1st level

Assessment Objectives		
5b	4	Save the slide show.
5c	5	Print each of the slides. Print each slide on a separate page.

TASK 3

This task is designed to allow you to practise the skills required to gain OCR Level 1 Certificate for IT Users (NEW CLAIT) assessment objectives.

Before you begin

You will need to find out and note down how to:

- delete text
- replace specified text
- promote/demote text
- print audience notes/thumbnails
- close a document.

What You Have To Do

Assessment Objectives		
4b, 4c, 4d 4e	1	You have been asked to make a few changes to the presentation:
	a	On slide 3, delete the item: **CHICKEN, PEANUT AND NOODLE SOUP**.
	b	On slide 3, add the following 2nd level item: **EGGPLANT AND LAMB RISOTTO**. Add it after **CURRY ONION NOODLES WITH EGG** and before **SABJI ONION CURRY**.
	c	On slide 3, demote the item **SABJI ONION CURRY** to become 2nd level text.
	d	Replace the word **ONION** with the word **COCONUT** wherever it appears in the presentation (3 times in all).
5b	2	Save the amended presentation show.
5d	3	Print a set of audience notes with 3 thumbnail slides per page.
1a, 5e	4	Close the presentation and exit the software securely.

Presentation Graphics Checklist

You should complete this checklist for each hardware and software combination you use. Use information from your tutor, handouts, handbooks and software manuals to complete the list. You can then use your list as a reference sheet to complete the practice tasks that follow.

Hardware: _____

Software: _____

ASSESSMENT OBJECTIVE	HOW TO DO IT	OCR REFERENCE
1 Identify and use appropriate software correctly		
Use appropriate application software	_____	1a
2 Set up a slide layout/template		
Create text areas/text frames	_____	2a
Apply background	_____	2b
Insert graphic	_____	2c
3 Format text style		
Use specified font sizes	_____	3a
Use bullets	_____	3b
Apply alignment	_____	3c
Apply enhancement	_____	3d
4 Enter and edit data		
Create a new slide	_____	4a
Insert text	_____	4b
Delete text	_____	4c
Replace specified text	_____	4d
Promote/demote text	_____	4e
5 Manage and print presentation files		
Create new presentation	_____	5a
Save document	_____	5b
Print slides	_____	5c
Print audience notes/thumbnails	_____	5d
Close document	_____	5e

OCR Assignments and Self-Assessments

This task allows you to practise a complete OCR Level 1 Certificate for IT Users (NEW CLAIT) assignment. It covers all the OCR Level 1 Certificate for IT Users (NEW CLAIT) presentation graphics assessment objectives.

You will need the image files **craftlogo** and **ringlogo**.

 You will find the **craftlogo** and **ringlogo** files on the CD supplied with this book.

Scenario

You work as an administrator for Craft Fairs International. You have been asked to produce a slide show presentation.

What You Have To Do

Assessment Objectives		
1a		**Your team leader has asked you to produce a short presentation of 3 slides.**
	1	Load application software that will allow you to produce a slide show presentation.
2a, 2b	2	Create or amend the master slide as follows:
2c, 3a, 3b	a	Create a page-wide **title** frame at the top of the page.
3c, 3d, 4b	b	Create a page-wide **main** frame below the title frame.
4e, 5a	c	Set up the text styles in these frames as follows:

Frame	Style	Emphasis	Size	Bullets	Alignment
title	title	bold only	40	no	centre
main	1st level	italic only	20	yes	left
main	2nd level	none	20	yes	left and indented

d Place the image **craftlogo** at the top left corner of the slide, and the image **ringlogo** at the bottom right corner of the slide. Make sure that they do not overlap the text frames.

e Create a frame at the bottom of the page, below the main frame. Enter your name, centre number and today's date in this frame.

f Format the background to be white.

What You Have To Do

Assessment Objectives		
5b	3	Save the master slide. This master slide is to be used for all 3 slides.
4a, 4b	4	Create slide 1 and enter the title: **FORTHCOMING EVENTS**
		Leave the main frame blank for this slide.
4a, 4b	5	Create slide 2 and enter the title: **FAIRS**

Enter the following text in the main frame, with the styles shown:

SPRING	1st level
CERAMIC ITEMS	1st level
LACE	1st level
LACQUER ITEMS	1st level
AUTUMN	1st level
EMBROIDERY	1st level
SILVERWARE	1st level
JEWELLERY ITEMS	1st level

Assessment Objectives		
4a, 4b	6	Create slide 3 and enter the title: **DEALERS**

Enter the following text in the main frame, with the styles shown:

UK	1st level
AMANDA NICHOLLS	2nd level
PAUL WHITTINGHAM	2nd level
USA	1st level
ENRICO GONZALES	2nd level
THOMAS CYRUS	2nd level
VIETNAM	1st level
NGUYEN THANH	1st level
HOAI TRANG	1st level

Assessment Objectives		
5b	7	Save the slide show.
5c	8	Print each of the slides. Print each slide on a separate page.
4b, 4c, 4d 4e	9	Your team leader has requested a few changes to the presentation:

a   On slide 2, delete the item: **SILVERWARE**

b   On slide 3, add the following name after **USA** and before **ENRICO GONZALES**:

    MARIANNA SCHWARTZ   2nd level

c   On slide 3, demote the names **NGUYEN THANH** and **HOAI TRANG** to become 2nd level text.

d   Replace the word **ITEMS** with the word **PRODUCTS** wherever it appears in the presentation (3 times in all).

Assessment Objectives		
5b	10	Save the amended presentation show.
5d	11	Print a set of audience notes with 3 thumbnail slides per page.
1a, 5e	12	Close the presentation and exit the software securely.

Self-assessment: Task 4

Did I do it correctly?

☐ Loaded application software to produce a slide show presentation

☐ Created the master slide as follows:
- created a page-wide **title** frame at the top of the page
- created a page-wide **main** frame below the title frame
- set up the text styles in these frames
- placed the image **craftlogo** at the top left corner of the slide, and the image **ringlogo** at the bottom right corner of the slide
- created a frame at the bottom of the page, below the main frame, and entered your name, centre number and the date in the frame
- formatted the background to be white

☐ Saved the master slide

☐ Created 3 slides as specified

☐ Saved the slide show

☐ Made the following changes:`
- deleted the item **SILVERWARE** on slide 2
- inserted **MARIANNA SCHWARTZ** (2nd level) on slide 3, after **USA** and before **ENRICO GONZALES**
- demoted **NGUYEN THANH** and **HOAI TRANG** to 2nd level text on slide 3
- replaced the word **ITEMS** with the word **PRODUCTS** (3 times in all)

☐ Saved the amended presentation

☐ Printed:
- each of the slides on a separate page
- a set of audience notes with 3 thumbnail slides per page

☐ Closed the presentation and exit the software securely

TASK 5

This task allows you to practise a complete OCR Level 1 Certificate for IT Users (NEW CLAIT) assignment. It covers all the OCR Level 1 Certificate for IT Users (NEW CLAIT) presentation graphics assessment objectives.

You will need the image file **weblogo**.

You will find the **weblogo** file on the CD supplied with this book.

Scenario

You work as an administrator for Progress Webs. You have been asked to produce a slide show presentation.

What You Have To Do

Assessment Objectives		
1a	1	**Your team leader has asked you to produce a short presentation of 3 slides.** Load application software that will allow you to produce a slide show presentation.
2a, 2b 2c, 3a, 3b 3c, 3d, 4b 4e, 5a	2	Create or amend the master slide as follows: a Create a page-wide **title** frame at the top of the page. b Create a page-wide **main** frame below the title frame. c Set up the text styles in these frames as follows:

Frame	Style	Emphasis	Size	Bullets	Alignment
title	title	italic only	40	no	left
main	1st level	bold only	24	yes	left
main	2nd level	none	24	yes	left and indented

d Place the image **weblogo** at the bottom left corner of the slide. Make sure that the logo does not overlap the text frames.

e Create a frame at the bottom of the page, below the main frame. Enter your name, centre number and today's date in this frame.

f Format the background to be white.

5b	3	Save the master slide. This master slide is to be used for all 3 slides.
4a, 4b	4	Create slide 1 and enter the title: **introducing the dynamic web** Leave the main frame blank for this slide.
4a, 4b	5	Create slide 2 and enter the title: **dynamic architecture design**

Enter the following text in the main frame, with the styles shown:

what is it?	1st level
interactivity is fundamental	2nd level
making movies	2nd level
the technology	1st level
java	2nd level
cgi	2nd level
shockwave	2nd level
gif animations	2nd level

4a, 4b	6	Create slide 3 and enter the title: **tools for web interactivity**

Enter the following text in the main frame, with the styles shown:

immediate in-screen feedback	1st level
dynamic multimedia	2nd level
dynamically generating content	1st level
random presentation	1st level
browser detection	2nd level
personalising content	2nd level

5b	7	Save the slide show.
5c	8	Print each of the slides. Print each slide on a separate page.

What You Have To Do

Assessment Objectives		
4b, 4c, 4d 4e	9	Your team leader has requested a few changes to the presentation: **a** On slide 3, delete the line: **browser detection** **b** On slide 3, add the following line after **immediate in-screen feedback** and before **dynamic multimedia**: **the animated image map** 2nd level **c** On slide 3, demote the line **random presentation** to become 2nd level text. **d** Replace the word **dynamic** with the word **interactive** wherever it appears in the presentation (3 times in all).
5b	10	Save the amended presentation show.
5d	11	Print a set of audience notes with 3 thumbnail slides per page.
5e	12	Close the presentation and exit the software securely.

Self-assessment: Task 5

Did I do it correctly?

- ☐ Used appropriate application software
- ☐ Created text areas/text frames
- ☐ Applied background
- ☐ Inserted a graphic
- ☐ Used specified font sizes
- ☐ Used bullets
- ☐ Applied alignment
- ☐ Applied enhancement
- ☐ Created frames
- ☐ Inserted text
- ☐ Deleted text
- ☐ Replaced specified text
- ☐ Demoted text
- ☐ Created a new presentation
- ☐ Saved the document
- ☐ Printed the slides
- ☐ Printed audience notes/thumbnails
- ☐ Closed the document.